**P L O U**

**P A**

Ploughboy and plough

Pastor and Pulpit

# PLOUGHBOY to PASTOR

By
David Obbard.
Sussex Farmer
and Pastor.

"I was a herdsman and gatherer of fruit.
Then the Lord took me...and said, 'Go'".

The family home at Cherry Gardens.

Remembrances of childhood days,
Of country scenes now passed and gone,
And through it all, God's wondrous ways,
Providing, teaching, leading on;
Just how He gave that gracious aid
Is in this little book displayed.

All rights reserved.
Copyright © 1991 David Obbard.
Cherry Gardens Publications,
Groombridge, Tunbridge Wells,
Kent. TN3 9NY

ISBN 0 9517416 1 6

Pen and ink drawings by Sue Obbard.

By the same author; 'Countryman's Heritage'
Spiritual lessons drawn from country scenes
and the author's own experiences.

## CONTENTS

| | |
|---|---|
| Author's Foreword. | page 7 |
| The Ploughboy. | 9 |
| A Good Hope Through Grace. | 21 |
| The Love of God. | 33 |
| Call to the Ministry. | 41 |
| Immersion in the Spirit. | 51 |
| A Minister of the Gospel. | 57 |
| Vision or Dream? | 75 |
| Rehoboth. | 83 |
| New Beginnings. | 97 |
| Appendix. | 109 |
| | |
| Poems; Arise my Love. | 40 |
| The Runaway Horse. | 42 |

## ILLUSTRATIONS

| | |
|---|---|
| Pony and Trap. | 8 |
| Two Brothers. | 12 |
| Forest Fold Sunday School. | 14 |
| The Chicken Thief. | 19 |
| The Young Ploughboy. | 22 |
| The Runaway Horse. | 45 |
| Forest Fold Chapel. | 47 |
| Smart's Hill Chapel. | 50 |
| Lamberhurst Chapel. | 56 |
| Caterham Chapel. | 72 |
| Rehoboth Chapel. | 84 |
| A Load of Mischief. | 90 |
| Ploughing with Prince. | 100 |

## TO MY MOTHER

Who first set my feet on the path of prayer, and whose self-sacrificial love was appreciated more as the years went by. We were privileged to have her die in our home, "as a bride prepared to be adorned for her husband". In those last days there was but one name on her lips, "Jesus", and her last words were, "He has come".

## AUTHOR'S FOREWORD

IT WAS the Roman statesman, Marcus Porcius Cato, who, whenever he made a speech, whatever the subject, always ended it with the words, "Delenda est Carthago" - Carthage must be destroyed. I have a friend who, whenever I meet him, whatever the occasion, will say, "Have you begun writing your memoirs yet?" - presumably adopting Cato's tactics!

This book is not my memoirs, but it does contain a mixture of incidents from my own life, and some very interesting features of a way of life that is now gone. Certain theological arguments are advanced in it, and as the author is a "nonconformist Nonconformist", the reader may find a few things to ponder over and examine in the light of scripture.

The following pages result from an urge to recall and record God's goodness in the events and experiences of my life up to the early years of my pastorate of the church meeting at Rehoboth Strict Baptist Chapel, Tunbridge Wells, and from a desire to urge upon believers the scriptural truth that whoever sincerely calls Jesus Christ Lord is a member of the body of Christ - as taught in First Corinthians 12, particularly verse 13, "For by one Spirit are we all baptised into one body."

Some years ago a relative of mine was explaining to her little daughter that great changes were about to come into her life because her husband had been sent out to preach. She said, "Daddy will no longer be with us on Sundays, but if just one soul is saved it will be worth it." To her amazement and joy the little one answered, "If only one soul is <u>helped</u> it will be worthwhile, won't it?" It is in that same spirit that I send out this little book.

Cherry Gardens,
Groombridge,
1991.

My father and his three sons in the pony trap. Topsy, the pony, was a real 'Black Beauty'. Beside being used in the trap for transporting the family, she did invalueable work in the market garden and fruit beds. There she pulled the 'shim', a horse-hoe that could be adjusted for various widths and needs.

# CHAPTER 1
# THE PLOUGHBOY

FRUSTRATED BY the obdurate refusal of the priests and theologians of his day to accept the teaching of the word of God instead of the dogmatics of a decadent Church, Tyndale once said, when in dispute with a certain learned man: "I defy the pope and all his laws; if God spare my life, ere many years I will cause a boy that driveth a plough shall know more of the Scripture than thou dost."

This ploughboy, the third of three sons, was born into the family of a smallholder struggling to make a living out of a few acres in the lean years which brought penury to agriculture following the First World War of 1914-1918. The first son, William, was afflicted in such a way that he could never follow in his father's footsteps, and the second, Joseph, so brilliant academically that his mother vowed he would never spend his life working for nothing as she and her husband had done. So it was automatically assumed that I, who had a remarkably strong physical frame, an aptitude for all things practical, and an inability to pass exams at school, would be the one to carry on the family tradition and follow the plough.

My school days were spent at the same little Church of England elementary school as my mother had attended. Little had changed during the intervening years: I sat on the same seats as she had done, and used some of the same textbooks. We met in a building which, I believe, was originally a Chapel of Ease before Groombridge became a parish and had a church of its own. As in my mother's day, it was divided into three parts by folding partitions: classes 1-3 under an infant teacher, classes 4-5 under a head mistress, and classes 6-7 under the headmaster. Any child who progressed through the school curriculum before leaving school at fourteen moved into X7 and had a certain amount of additional teaching, but was expected to get on without supervision. In my mother's day these children were expected to help with the little ones as "pupil teachers".

The lessons were very much orientated towards preparing us for the type of work country children were expected to go into. For instance, in arithmetic we had to compute the tonnage in haystacks of different dimensions. This varied according to whether the hay was "new", i.e. freshly made, or "old", i.e. well settled down at the end of the winter - the latter being heavier per cubic foot. New methods and subjects were also included, and the teachers were dedicated to their profession, so that the standard of education was good. Not all the real country folk were in agreement with changes, and I remember being told of one old lady who said, "Readin' an' writin' an' sums is all right, but this 'ere arithmetic, that ain't no good to them."

One thing which had radically changed was the church itself. From being a very "Low" church it had become a "High" church, with a priest, or a "Father", in charge. As Nonconformists we were not allowed by our parents, nor expected by the teachers, to take part in worship within the church, although receiving the same religious instruction at the school. Whenever the other children went to a church service we were put together in one classroom, and left on our honour to get on without supervision at whatever work we had been set.

The headmistress was a devout believer, very active in the church and Sunday school, and an accomplished musician and singing teacher. Towards the end of my school life two "Sisters of Mercy" from an Anglican convent had a mission at the school, with services in the church. To the great disapproval of some of my fellow Nonconformist scholars, I went to these services. The next week, for composition in English, we had to write about their visit, and I began my article with, "As John the Baptist heralded the coming of the Lord Jesus, so leaflets and handbills heralded the coming of the Sisters of Mercy." This dear soul was so pleased about it, that I believe she thought she had made a convert! She was still at the school when I sent my own children there twentyfive years later.

Even as a child I was well versed in the old Authorised Version of the Bible, and although we were never taught grammar, as in the Secondary Schools, this knowledge of the Bible gave me a good understanding of correct English. It also had what now seems an amusing effect on my "Composition". On one occasion we were told to write a letter applying for a job. The headmaster was highly delighted to find I had concluded mine with the words, "If I find grace in thy sight, I will serve you to the best of my ability." I was asked to re-write the letter in my best handwriting for him to keep and show to his friends!

So I was privileged to grow up in a rural setting, not so very different from that which my parents had known. Healthy, happy and free, we roamed the fields and woods without the fears and dangers which surround children today. Although not very proficient in organised sports, I was a good runner, very strong physically, somewhat below average height, and quite capable of holding my own when it came to blows. However, my parental upbringing ensured I was honest, kind toward the weak, and possessed with a strong sense of justice.

The last could sometimes create problems, as when I climbed up the tall roof of our house to retrieve an arrow which had lodged behind the chimney stack. On reaching the ground I found my father waiting to tan my backside with the selfsame arrow for my misdeed. I felt doubly hurt, for I had never been told I must not climb up the roof! When I look at that roof now, I don't wonder at my father's handling of the matter: I only wonder how it was I did not slip and break my neck. This was

My brother Joe (on the right) and myself in our late teens, just before he volunteered for the RAF. He trained as an Observer in Canada, and was offered a post as instructor in Astro Navigation, but declined saying it was a job for those who had done their period of bombing missions.

one of the many escapades in which I now see the protecting hand of a loving heavenly Father.

Another occasion comes to mind of God's providential care over me. My brother Joe and I were keen collectors of bird's eggs. We had watched a crow's nest being built in the top of a very tall, slender tree growing in a wood about a mile from our home, and when we judged the eggs were laid, I climbed the tree to get one for our collection. To my horror, just as I was getting within reach of the nest, the tree began to droop over at the top under my weight, tipping the eggs out of the nest, and leaving me hanging on for life, suspended seemingly in space. Fortunately I dropped into the top of a near-by thorn tree, which, although not comfortable, saved me from serious injury.

As in most country chapels in my boyhood days, there were many children of roughly the same age, many of them closely related to one another, as movement, even between villages, was very restricted, and many marriages took place within the community of the same church or chapel. These young people usually formed into groups according to age, and, except for a cousin who was born a few days after me, I was the youngest in the group to which I was attached. Although youngest and smallest - or perhaps because of it - I was ever anxious to be in the forefront of any activity that was going on. I well remember my grandfather laying hold of me one Sunday as he thought I was on some dubious business, and demanding to know what I was up to. His light blue eyes seemed to look right through me as he said, "You are Satan's chief agent among the boys". We all had our midday meal together in the chapel following the morning service, and if the weather was fine we went for a walk through the fields and woods or country lanes in the interval between this and Sunday School. This was a welcome interlude in what we considered a very boring and restricted day. At such times high spirits were often

The Old Sunday School at Forest Fold.

The school was on the first floor, and entrance was by way of the stairs seen on the left. The ground floor now houses a toilet block. The large door on the left side gave access to the coach house; the other to the stables; Topsy was put there Sundays.

let loose in what I would call "innocent pranks". Alas, some things were not always innocent, and even now, fifty five years later, I am sometimes troubled by evil things I heard and learned on those Sunday walks. Obscene rhymes can be easily learnt, but not so easily forgotten.

However, as an example of the wayward things we did, let me recall a scene from the Sunday School. We received "marks" which were totalled up at the end of the year and by which the value of our book prize was calculated. There was one mark for each attendance, one for learning a text, and one for good conduct, so that if we were present at both services in the chapel, and both morning and after-noon Sunday School, we received six marks. We were also allowed to take a small picture text from a box each week, and this box was taken round the classes by the eldest son of the Superintendent at that time, a tall, elegant lad, the perfect example of good behaviour. One day, as he lifted the lid of the box and presented it to the primary class, out of it jumped a huge yellow frog. The pandemonium which followed was hilarious! The sight of this young lad emulating the frog as he hopped after it up the central aisle of the Sunday School, still clutching the ticket box in one hand, and vainly endeavouring to catch the offending creature with the other, sent the whole school into fits of laughter - all, that is, except the teacher of my class. He seized me by the shoulder and said grimly, "Did you put that in there?" - and then, hardly waiting for an answer, continued, "It's not too late to take off your mark for good conduct." (I thought at the time this was unfair. My conduct in the Sunday School was at that time exemplary. It was not I who had let the frog out, I had only put it in the box, and that was during the dinner-time interlude.)

My upbringing was a mixture of rigidity and liberty - but not the undisciplined freedom of the 1980's. No work was done on the Sunday other than that which was necessary for looking after the livestock. No playing cards were allowed, although we were allowed many other card games. No going to the pictures, dance halls, pantomimes, fairs or circus. On the other hand, we were instructed in the use of a 12-bore shotgun, at which we became adept before school leaving age. I remember a gentleman giving my brother a whole sixpence because he was so delighted to see Joe bring down a starling in full flight as it was homing in on a cherry tree.

One exception to the "no work on Sunday" rule was birdscaring during the cherry picking season. There were no other cherry orchards within miles of our own, and it seemed as if all the birds in East Sussex made their way to us as soon as the fruit began to ripen. Every morning, including Sunday, someone was on duty as soon as it was light, as if left unmolested for just one day, the birds were capable of stripping the trees of fruit. The blackbirds and thrushes would break off a cherry and fly away to eat it, but the great flocks of starlings simply sat on the twigs gorging themselves with the fruit, leaving the stones on the "cherry strigs" like skeletons. Sometimes a whole flock of rooks would descend on the orchard, and what havoc they could wreak in a short time!

Sometimes we might be troubled by a particularly persistent and wily bird, especially in the currant and raspberry beds. These were controlled by special cage-like traps, which held the birds captive without injuring them, and if a song thrush, or one of the more beneficial birds were caught by mistake, we would release it. Recalling such an incident in later years when composing recitations for Sunday School work, I used it as an illustration:

A fowler set his snare
With cherries for a bait;
As it was sited with great care
He had not long to wait.

A thrush came hopping by,
For breakfast he'd had nought;
The bright red cherries caught his eye,
And soon he too was caught.

But see! a friend comes near
Who loves the birds that sing;
The way to freedom soon is clear:
Once more he's on the wing.
Now listen to his lay
While singing on the tree:
I'm free, I'm free, he seems to say,
I'm free! I'm free! I'm FREE!

And that is how I felt
When Jesus set me free;
He showed me all my sinful debt
Was paid at Calvary.
I'm free, I'm free, I'm FREE:
Yet I am not my own:
Since Jesus gave his life for me,
My life is His alone.

One Sunday, while birdscaring, I saw three wild duck disappear among the trees surrounding a pond on land my father rented as grazing for his horses and few cows. Leaving my post I quickly made my way there, and, stealthily crawling through the woody undergrowth like some big-game hunter, was able to bag all three with my double-barrelled shotgun. That episode got me into trouble, for I learned that while it was legitimate to use the gun in protecting the fruit, stalking ducks was "breaking the Sabbath" - this was seeking my own pleasure on God's holy day (Isaiah 58 v13).

Looking back, I see that I later imposed a similar pattern of upbringing on my own children. One Sunday morning when my son did not know what to do with himself, my wife said, "Why don't you go up to the farm and help your father with the cows?

He has so much to do, and I am sure he would be glad of your help; there is plenty you could do." She received the terse reply, "If I'm not allowed to play on Sunday, I'm certainly not going to work!"

My wife was brought up much more strictly than I was, and in bringing up our family we both had to adjust in order not to undermine each other's authority. Such situations were not uncommon among the families of my generation. One minister I know said, "My wife, as a girl, was not allowed to set her foot on the pier when at the seaside; my mother took me on the pier, and gave me pennies to put in the slot machines" - selected ones, of course! Another friend told me that, living by the seaside, they walked along the seashore almost every day of the week, but were never permitted to do so on a Sunday. On Sunday afternoon they were taken for a walk in the park! Even this could have its problems, for I had it on good authority that such a walk once cost a pastor his position. Out for a walk with his wife one bright Sunday afternoon, they were caught in a heavy thunderstorm and ran for shelter. The only shelter available was near the bandstand, where they were spotted by someone from the church, and he was dismissed for breaking the Sabbath by listening to worldly music in an ungodly crowd.

As children we received no pocket money; in fact, in common with many boys in similar circumstances, I received no wages when first leaving school and working at home. We were, however, given a plot of land to cultivate for ourselves, and we obtained money from other sources. In the spring we picked primroses and made up little bunches of these lovely flowers, each bunch having a ring of leaves round the outside. Later on, we would pick blackberries and mushrooms, scouring a large area of the countryside. Then through the winter we went rabbiting, ridding our own and some of our neighbour's land of these pests for our profit. We also caught foxes, skinning them and sending away the pelts to a London firm. Foxes were, and still are, a menace to free range hens, and so my father was glad to get rid of them, and delighted to have their carcasses to boil up with potatoes etc. in his copper, providing food for the hens. "That," he would say, "is a case of the biter being bit."

The Chicken Thief.

Throughout all these activities there was a realisation that God truly was, and that somehow he was involved in our lives. Not only did we hear of him in home, chapel and school, but we were aware of his Being in the world of nature around us. There is a sense in which it has been rightly said, "We are nearer God's heart in a garden than anywhere else on earth." In those days, before mechanisation and commercialisation changed our countryside so dramatically, we truly lived in "the Garden of England", although geographically two miles south of the Kent and Sussex border.

By the time I was eleven, I could plough a reasonable furrow, milk a cow, and pick strawberries faster than most of the eight to ten casual pickers who were employed by my father in the summer months. Small wonder that when the few hectic weeks of the fruit picking season arrived, I was often absent from school: neither did I find it irksome to be free from the desk, picking cherries from a long ladder in the trees that were planted by my grandfather, or doing whatever task might have been appointed me.

I well remember my parents getting a visit from the School Inspector, who examined the school one Friday and discovered, not only that I was absent, but also that such absence was no uncommon occurrence. The next week he arrived in a taxi (we lived two miles from the school and station), and had the misfortune to meet my mother instead of my father. His pompous and authoritative demands to know why I was absent from school on the previous Friday, and other occasions, was met with a mild question: "If my son was absent on Friday, why did you not come to see me on Friday?" His indignant reply, "Why, madam, you surely could not expect me to walk all that way after I had spent all day in the school" was met with another quiet question: "If you could not walk it once, how do you expect my son to walk it five times a week?" Seeing the glint of battle in her eye, and noting the steel in the quiet voice, he simply said, "Well madam, send him as often as you can"; which is what my parents did.

When I left school at 14, I was keen to take up an opportunity to go to the county Agricultural College at Plumpton. My father was reluctant to let me go, and being told by a neighbouring farmer, "All they will teach him there is how to lose money", he said, "I can teach him how to do that here". I was present at that conversation, and it spelled the end of my formal education.

## CHAPTER 2
## A GOOD HOPE THROUGH GRACE

NOT All education however takes place in school or college, and not all of our education relates to the things of this material world, so that I see now that even before my school days were ended, God had begun to educate me for the task he had in mind.

Perhaps the first lesson I remember concerned prayer. My brothers and I used to walk the two and a half miles from our home to Sunday School at the Forest Fold Baptist Chapel, Crowborough, every Lord's Day morning, and many were the adventures I can recall connected with that practice. One particularly stands out in my memory.

By the side of what was a remote country road stood a house with a small shop in the front, where a widow sold a variety of provisions. One particular Sunday my attention was drawn to a number of chalk-written notices: "Tea sold here: Sugar sold here: Honey sold here" etc.. It dawned on me that this last notice could be improved, and digging among the contents of my jacket pocket I produced a piece of chalk with which I expertly altered it to "Money sold here".

My brother Joe suddenly said, "Hey, give me the chalk," and going up to the door, wrote in bold letters, "Filth sold here". We had our laugh before proceeding on our way, and the incident was quickly forgotten among the multitude of other matters which fill a schoolboy's mind and time. It was however sharply brought to mind later in the week, when my father answered a knock at the door and found the local policeman who had come to make some inquiries. Had my father gone to chapel on Sunday? Yes. Did he notice anything written on Clark's shop door? No, but the boys might have seen something!

Had we seen anything written on the door? Yes. Did we know who put it there? Yes, we had written

The Young Ploughboy.
with his two favourite horses.

it for a lark. Now this was a keen young policeman, eager to earn his stripes, and we learned that the owner of the shop had had words with a dissatisfied customer just previous to that Sunday morning, and, being convinced it was he who had written the offensive notice, had called the police, intent on making a court case of it.

My parents conferred, and Father went off on his bicycle to make amends to the offended party. We eagerly awaited his return, but our hearts fell as he entered the house with a heavy foot and heavier heart. He said that the good woman had already promised the policeman that if he found the culprit she would prosecute: it was out of her hands, and there was little hope that the police would drop the case.

My mother looked meaningfully at me and said, "Well, you know what you've got to do now, don't you." Yes, I knew what I had got to do, and quickly made my way to a little out-building where I would be certain of not being disturbed, and on my knees poured out my heart to God.

I remember still the content of that prayer, and the earnest way in which I pleaded with God. At that time I knew nothing of the way of salvation, or why we prayed "for Jesus' sake", but I knew from the Bible that the God of Abraham was a God who could, and did, answer prayer, One who could do the impossible. And so it was to the God of Abraham, Isaac and Jacob that I prayed. The burden of that prayer was simply this, that not only would it bring shame and reproach upon my parents, but on the chapel, and upon the name of God himself. Although I was only a child, I learned that day what it was to pray, "For Thy great name's sake".

Anxious days followed, but when the policeman called again, he simply said, "I've decided not to pursue the case against the boys." As soon as I heard the good news I went with eager steps to my 'secret place' and poured out my heart in gratitude to God who had "heard the voice of the lad" as surely as he had heard the voice of Ishmael, Abram's son by Hagar, as he lay under the bush in the wilderness of Beer-sheba (Genesis 21; v 17).

Another thing I learnt in the school of God while still a young boy was his holiness, his anger against sin, and the reality of hell. 'Our seat' at the little Baptist chapel went L-shaped round two sides of the Tortoise stove which was the only means of heating the building during the winter time. We sang lustily, as all good Baptists did in those days: "The treble sweet, the tenor bold, the flute-like alto rare as gold, and deep resounding bass." I cannot honestly say I remember what we were singing on that particular Sunday, though in after years, upon reflection, I think it could have been:
"Lord, should thy judgements grow severe,
I am condemned, but thou art clear.
Should sudden vengeance seize my breath
I must pronounce thee just in death;
And if my soul were sent to hell,
Thy righteous law approves it well."

What I do vividly remember is that the old Tortoise stove had disappeared from my sight, and I felt to stand on the very brink of a blazing inferno. It was so real, as if I actually saw it with my eyes. I was transfixed, and only brought back to reality when my father looked down to see what mischief I was up to instead of singing. Then all I could do was to gaze round the chapel and wonder how it was possible that people could sing such dreadful words with such gusto and apparent unconcern.

Although the deep and sobering impression this vision made upon me was soon lost, the remembrance of it was something which never left me entirely, even in the days when later I sought to out-swear my school companions to prove I did not deserve the name of "Bible Puncher" with which I was sometimes taunted because I went to chapel.

Perhaps it was partly this experience which caused me to react badly against teaching I received from well-meaning Sunday School teachers and preachers, which came over to me as, "If you don't love God, he will send you to hell when you die." I am sure that is not what they meant to convey, and doubtless the love of God and the way of salvation were clearly and patiently explained; but nothing of true gospel teaching seemed to register.

One other thing, I remember, made a great impression on my mind at that time. In our school hymnbook I discovered this hymn:

My God I love thee, not because
I hope for heaven thereby!
Nor because they who love thee not
Are lost eternally.

Thou, O my Jesus, thou didst me
Upon the cross embrace;
For me didst bear the nails and spear,
And manifold disgrace;

And griefs and torments numberless,
And sweat of agony,
E'en death itself; and all for one
Who was thine enemy.

Then why, O blessed Jesus Christ,
Should I not love thee well?
Not for the sake of winning heaven,
Or of escaping hell;

Not for the sake of gaining aught,
Or seeking a reward;
But as thyself hast loved me,
O ever loving Lord.

> E'en so I love thee and will love,
> And in thy praise will sing;
> Solely because thou art my God
> And my eternal King.
> 
> Francis Xavier 1506 -52.

I remember thinking, "Well, if ever I become religious, that's the sort of religion that would appeal to me". As I had been brought up in a very anti-Roman Catholic environment, I think this too was part of my spiritual education in the days when I was unaware of God's hand upon my life.

The headmaster of the village school I attended was also an influence for good in my boyhood days. Although often administering the cane in an effort to "bring some good out of you", as he was wont to say, he would also take me aside at times and talk very seriously but kindly about the great issues of life. He was a big man in every way, and had seen much of life, being engaged in the battle of Jutland in the First World War and invalided out of the navy at the age of 16. When forced to teach evolution in the school curriculum, he emphasised that this was an unproven theory, He also said to me privately, "If I have to teach boys they die like animals, I shall expect that when they grow up they will live like animals." We have only to look in our daily papers to see how prophetically true those words were.

My teenage years were spent in hard but rewarding work on the land, which left me little time for anything else. Spiritually they were a time of alternating turmoil and apathy. In later years I read the life of John Newton, in which it was said there was a time when he blasphemed the name of God by day, and lay in terror of his holy law by night; a description that would often have been applicable to me. There were times when I walked up and down the road in the small hours of the morning, because I feared that if I went to sleep I would wake up in

Hell; at other times there was not a thought of God, and I was glad of any excuse to avoid going to chapel with my parents. If it had not been for my interest in a certain young lady who worshipped regularly, I probably would have left off altogether.

When all my good resolves came to nothing, and all my prayers to know my sins forgiven appeared unanswered, I concluded I was not one of "the elect", and decided to volunteer for the Navy and get away from it all. On going to the Labour Exchange, I was told that as a key worker on the land (it was at the time when the German U-boats appeared to be winning the war in the Atlantic), there was little prospect of my being freed, and as a member of the Home Guard I was probably doing more good where I was. This was another area in which I now see the Lord's overruling hand, as my brother, who was not tied in the same way as I was, had volunteered for the RAF and was one who later lost his life in action. The lines of the hymn which say, "Determined to save, he watched o'er my path, When Satan's blind slave I sported with death", have a very real meaning for me, as I reconsider those days.

Living as we did in "Bomb Alley" we saw plenty of action in the sky during the Battle of Britain, and in the London bombing. Often while at work spent bullets and empty cartridge shells would come scattering across the field, and occasionally a cannon shell from a German bomber would explode if it hit the hard ground. One night four bombs dropped on our own little holding, and the blast from the nearest one blew a cartshed close to our house out of perpendicular. It remained in that queer leaning position until the great wind of October 17th 1987, one more reminder of God's preserving care.

When London was subjected to dreadful bombing in the Blitz, there were some nights when the fires were clearly visible from our vantage point on a hill top. One evening as a German bomber fell out of the sky in a mass of flames I was whooping with delight. Then I turned, and saw my mother with tears in her eyes. She had a strange faraway look on her face. In reply to my inquiring look she said quietly, "They are all some mother's sons: one day it might be Joe." I now wonder if some German mother shed a tear for my brother Joe when his time came, and he was shot out of the sky over eastern Germany.

In my late teens and early twenties I was very much troubled about the doctrine of election. It was a doctrine strongly held among the people with whom I worshipped, and it became to me a matter of great concern. I wanted to know if I was among those chosen of God unto eternal life. It was not only the teaching of the scripture which convinced me of the truth of election, but the inability to produce anything of a spiritual nature of myself. I was well aware of the experience expressed in the hymn:

>This is the way I long have sought,
>And mourned because I found it not;
>My grief and burden long has been
>Because I could not cease from sin.
>The more I strove against its power,
>I sinned and stumbled but the more-

As yet I knew nothing of the rest of the hymn:

>Till late I heard my Saviour say,
>"Come hither soul, I am the way."
>Lo, glad I come, and thou, blest Lamb
>Will take me to thee as I am;
>Nothing but sin I thee can give;
>Nothing but love shall I receive.

In those days we seldom bought meat from the butcher, relying upon what could be caught in the wild, or the occasional chicken that had reached the end of its egg laying life. One day when out with the gun looking for a rabbit or some other game for dinner, and pondering over my spiritual state, I noticed a thorn bush some distance ahead, set out in the field away from the hedgerow I was working along, and I remember praying something like this: "Lord, if I am one of the elect, let there be a pheasant in that little bush."

As I approached the bush, I watched it keenly to see if anything flew out, or, as was more likely, silently slipped away through the grass. On coming up to it I looked carefully through the leaves and the long grass that grew up around it, but could see nothing. Then I gave the bush an exasperated kick, and out flew a pheasant! I was so surprised that although it rose in the air, a perfect target as it flew away from me, I never even lifted the gun. Neither did I have any feeling that this was an answer to my prayer, or a confirmation of my election. I then realised that if I was among the Lord's people, that knowledge would have to come some other way.

In 1945, on my twenty-third birthday, I married the girl who had already been an influence for good in my life, and who was to be used of God in the formation of my christian life and character more than any other individual. She was soon demobbed from the Wrens, and as we started our married life together, we also began earnestly to seek the Lord. We were privileged to be able to sit under a good ministry, both in my home chapel at Forest Fold, and in hers at Rehoboth, Tunbridge Wells, so that for a time we alternated between the two for our Sunday worship.

It was however through the hymns that I first received any personal encouragement and spiritual enlightenment. The words:

There were ninety and nine that safely lay
In the shelter of the fold,
But one was out on the hills away,
Far off from the gates of gold,

heard over the radio on one Sunday morning, stirred my soul to the depths. I was that one "away on the

mountains wild and bare, away from the tender Shepherd's care". Some insight into the Saviour's sufferings came to me through the another verse:
> But none of the ransomed ever knew
> How deep were the waters crossed;
> Nor how dark was the night that the Lord passed through
> Ere he found his sheep that was lost.

How I longed to know that the verse of the Shepherd's return would be true of me:
> But all through the mountains, thunder riven,
> And up from the rocky steep,
> There arose a cry to the gate of heaven,
> Rejoice! I have found my sheep!

The first sermon that I remember ever having real meaning to me was also on this subject, and about the same time. Mr. Brooker, the pastor of Rehoboth chapel, was preaching from the clause in John 10 v16, "Them also I must bring." As he described the "other sheep", and emphasised that only the Good Shepherd could bring them, but that he <u>would</u> bring them, I had my first experience of having my heart warmed under the preaching. I left the chapel that day with what would have been described among those worshippers as "a good hope through grace"; that the Good Shepherd would, one day, bring me rejoicing into the fold.

Although in a family that loved singing, often spending hours round the organ singing hymns, especially from "Sacred Songs and Solos", the first hymn I remember singing "with the heart and understanding" was Number 1075 in Gadsby's Selection:

> Thou hidden love of God, whose height,
> Whose depth unfathomed, no man knows,
> I see from far thy beauteous light,
> And inly sigh for thy repose;
> My heart is pained, nor can it be
> At rest, till it find rest in thee.

As we sang these words it suddenly dawned on me that this was exactly where I was in my search for God. What I was singing was the desire of my heart, and from that time the singing of hymns took on a new meaning for me. Although we cannot tell the measure of spirituality in the worship of others, I must confess that it grieves me to see and hear when hymns are sung without due emphasis on meaning and punctuation.

There is a story of some old monks who, realising that their own voices were no longer tuneful, trained a choir of young boys to sing the praises of God. So beautiful was the singing on the first day when the boys performed this function, that the Abbot was amazed to have a visit that night from an angel who asked, "Why was there no singing today?" He replied, "Oh, but there was, it was beautiful." The angel shook his head sadly and said, "It never reached heaven." I wonder how much of our singing goes no further than the sound of our voices!

Many times my voice had been used in singing and gone no further than the chapel walls, but I am sure that on that Sunday it rose to heaven, for not only was the first verse my experience, but in a very real way the rest of the hymn became my prayer - it still is today:

Is there a thing beneath the sun,
That strives with thee my heart to share?
Ah! tear it thence, and reign alone,
And govern every motion there.
Then shall my heart from earth be free,
When it has found its all in thee.

O crucify this self, that I
No more, but Christ in me, may live;
Bid all my vile affections die,
Nor let one hateful lust survive.
In all things nothing may I see,
Nothing desire, or seek, but thee.

> Lord, draw my heart from earth away,
> And make it only know thy call:
> Speak to my inmost soul and say,
> "I am thy Saviour, God, thy All!"
> O dwell in me, fill all my soul,
> And all my powers by thine control.

Much blessing did I receive through the singing of such hymns, and I believe it has been rightly said, "The theology of a church is largely shaped by the hymns it sings." How important it is that our hymns should contain good scriptural teaching as well as expressing the spiritual experience, prayers, and praises of the worshippers. The singing of hymns should not only be an expression of praise to God, but a means of building up believers in their faith, thus promoting further praise to Him. "Let the word of Christ dwell in you richly in all wisdom, teaching and admonishing one another in psalms and hymns and spiritual songs, singing with grace in your hearts to the Lord"(Colossians 3 v16). I had been convinced of sin, led to believe in the Saviour, built up in the faith, and given a good hope of being a child of God by the singing of hymns during the normal course of worship. Some speak lightly of a 'Hymn Sandwich' type of service, but they should remember that a meat sandwich is nourishing food, much better than some of the 'junk food' which is consumed today.

Following this revelation of truth in the singing of hymns I was greatly encouraged by hearing a sermon preached by Mr. Stanley Delves on Song of Solomon, chapter 2 v17: "Until the day break, and the shadows flee away, turn, my beloved, and be thou like a roe or a young hart upon the mountains of Bether." How my soul was stirred that evening, and drawn out to the Lord in anticipation of a blessed daybreak. Many insurmountable mountains intervened between me and the Lord, but I was assured that he would, in his own time and way, come skipping over them (v. 8), dispelling the shadows, and bringing light, gladness, and a new day into my heart.

## CHAPTER 3
## THE LOVE OF GOD

MY SOUL was now on tiptoe, expecting to have an experience such as John Newton describes in one of his hymns – some vision of the Lord Jesus hanging on the cross, and speaking peace and pardon to my soul. Indeed, I was saying to myself that nothing else would ever meet my need, satisfy my longing, or give me assurance that my sins were forgiven. It will come as no surprise to those who know much of the Lord's dealings, that my expectations and hopes were not fulfilled in the way that I anticipated, nor to know that those spiritual desires declined, and that instead of blessings I began to experience barrenness and at times almost apathy. "Hope deferred maketh the heart sick," and I became discouraged. Although a number of young people, some of whom were my close cousins, came forward for baptism in the spring and early summer of 1947, I felt little spiritual life, and certainly no thought of following the Lord in that ordinance, until one Sunday in September, which I will endeavour to recall in some detail.

This particular Sunday we cycled to chapel as usual, but I went simply as a matter of routine in the company of my wife, who had known something of the Lord Jesus when a girl in her teens, and whose conscience was more tender, and spiritual life more evident than my own. I remember so clearly sitting in the rear seat of the gallery and listening unconcernedly while our pastor preached from "God commandeth all men everywhere to repent". I was conscious that my heart was as hard as the seat on which I sat, and feeling somewhat justified in it, because the preacher knew that I could not produce repentance of myself. God knew that too, and yet he had not answered my prayers for the blessings I had so earnestly sought.

What happened to me that morning was something I could not and cannot find words to express, only this I know, God was pleased to shed abroad his love in my heart by the Holy Spirit which is given to us (Romans 5 v5). It was at that time unsought, unexpected, totally undeserved, and as far as I could see in no way related to what was being said by the preacher. However, one of the effects of this experience was that it wrought true repentance in my heart. My conscience was made tender, my love was drawn out to the Lord, and I proved that there is nothing like 'a sense of blood bought pardon to disolve the heart of stone'. The nearest I could approach to describing what I felt, was to say it was like having a healing and soothing ointment spread over a sunburnt skin. It was 'Joy unspeakable and full of glory', and affected me physically in that I could scarce walk, or ride my bicycle home.

Many years later I read of such an experience described by Mr. McKenzie, one time joint editor of the Gospel Standard, when preaching from Ephesians 1 v13-14 on the sealing of the Spirit. Nowhere else have I found words which better describe what I felt that day, but even the words of so gracious and gifted a man cannot adequately convey what it is to be immersed in the Love of Christ. We sometimes sang "Sink into that sea outright, Lose myself in Jesus quite", and that day I had my first experience of it.

How I praise God that he so sovereignly and graciously answered the prayers and desires he had earlier implanted in my heart according to his own word, to do "exceeding abundantly above all that we ask or think"! That was an unforgettable day: I walked out in the fields that afternoon savouring the wonder expressed in Wesley's hymn,

Love divine, all loves excelling,
Joy of heaven, to earth come down:
Fix in us thy humble dwelling,
All thy faithful mercies crown;

> Jesus, thou art all compassion;
> Pure, unbounded love thou art;
> Visit us with thy salvation;
> Enter every trembling heart.

The joy of heaven had truly entered my poor, trembling heart. To my faithful little Welsh collie, who looked questioningly up into my tear-filled eyes, I said, "Flossie, there was a time when I envied you because you had no soul to lose; now I know a wondrous satisfaction that you can never know." That scene is etched in my memory as clearly as if it had been only yesterday. Heaven above was brighter blue, earth beneath was fairer green, and my soul was full of wonder, love and praise.

One of the things which filled me with amazement that day was the eternal nature of the love of God. In some way which I could not explain it was conveyed to my soul that God had loved me from before the foundation of the world. Although I am not aware that the scripture came to my mind at that moment, I knew that God had said of me, "I have loved thee with an everlasting love, therefore with lovingkindness have I drawn thee". In the enjoyment of that love I knew that my sins were removed as far as the east is from the west, while peace, pardon, blessed assurance and joy took possession of my soul. That day the Spirit bore witness with my spirit that I was a child of God, and I knew what it was to have an earnest of the eternal inheritance purchased for us by our Saviour. Earnest is a term taken from an old-time custom in trading. It was a small sample of what had been purchased, which was at the same time a guarantee that the rest would follow. For the first time I could truly sing with Watts:

> Beneath his smiles my soul has lived,
> And part of heaven possessed;
> I'll praise his name for grace received,
> And trust him for the rest.

My one desire now was to follow the Lord in baptism, and I resolved to see the pastor that night, to tell him what the Lord had done for my soul. Accordingly, I went to the Branch Chapel that evening on my own, and after the service cycled to the pastor's house intent on seeing him, expecting that he would be at home. However, he had decided to visit elsewhere, and as I sat on a seat outside, the chill of the evening seemed to affect my spirit, and instead of warmth of heart, a coldness and numbness of mind possessed me. It became dark, but I resisted the temptation to go home and say nothing, sensing that I was at a point of crisis, like that of the children of Israel at Kadesh Barnea. Not to go forward, despite the walled cities which now presented themselves to my mind, could well result in many more years in a spiritual wilderness.

When Mr. Delves came home and invited me into his study, I was totally confused and almost speechless. The only thing I remember is asking, "If I was a real Christian, wouldn't I want to go to heaven?" - for I seemed to possess no such desire. He countered this by asking, "Well, David, what do you desire?" I replied fervently, "I want to be <u>like Him</u>."

I was advised to go home, and when able, to write a letter; meanwhile, he promised to pray that the Holy Spirit would be my remembrancer, and that is exactly what happened. Over the next few days, although I was very busy attending to the threshing machine, the Holy Spirit took me step by step back over my life, showing me that "at sundry times and in divers manners" (some of which are recorded here) he had been speaking to me and leading me in the path of truth. As I recalled and recorded what the Lord had done for my soul I was surprised at my former blindness, and humbled under a sense of his graciousness and patience. I felt I could say, "God, who caused the light to shine out of darkness, has shined in (my) heart, to give the light of the knowledge of the glory of God in the face of Jesus Christ."

This was the time of my first love, and how applicable were the words of the Song of Solomon. "My beloved spake, and said unto me, Rise up, my love, my fair one, and come away. For lo, the winter is past, the rain is over and gone, the flowers appear on the earth; the time of the singing of birds is come, and the voice of the turtle is heard in our lands". For many days, even weeks, I went in the felt enjoyment of his love. My mother's father, who worked on the railway, was often ridiculed by his workmates for his faith in Christ. "How do you know that Jesus is alive today?" they would scoff. In his quiet way he would say, "I love him, and feel his love in my heart. I could not do that if he was not real". That experience had become mine, and I entered "The Sabbath of his love"(Gadsby's Hymns No 1061). Not only did I know that my sins were forgiven, but, in the joy of his salvation, sin itself was subdued, so that I walked in the light, having fellowship with God, proving that the blood of Jesus Christ cleanses from all sin.

The meaning of the term 'first love', as used in Revelation 2 v4, is not to be confined to that first revelation of love to a seeking soul, or that soul's response of love to the Lord Jesus. This is indeed a unique time in the experience of a believer, which is akin to the disciples' first experience of the risen Saviour. Those who have been brought up with the knowledge of Christ's resurrection will never be able to experience quite the same feelings of wonder and amazement that must have filled their breasts when they first saw him, but the first experience of having the love of God shed abroad in the heart by the Holy Spirit comes with something of that same amazing wonder. It is indescribable, and the effect is that the Lord Jesus becomes our first love. We love Him more than husband, wife, children or self, as he has required of those who would be his disciples. We lose our first love, not so much when the initial realization of that love wanes, but when anything else becomes more precious to us than the love and service of the Master.

When the believer sets out on his discipleship, he is like Peter stepping out of the boat on to the water, and walking to the Lord Jesus. It was his love <u>to</u> the Lord, and faith <u>in him</u>, that enabled Peter to venture out on a journey which was humanly impossible. While that faith and love centred on Christ to the exclusion of other considerations, he walked safely. When he took his eyes off the Saviour, 'when he saw the wind boisterous and was afraid', he began to sink. The treacherous nature of our hearts, which are as unstable as water, the boisterous wind of temptation, the storms of life, and the equally treacherous calm, make it that only as our faith is fixed on Jesus, and our love drawing us closer to him, can we truly live the christian life. When we leave our first love, that is to allow anything else to have prior claim upon our affections, we are as much in danger of sinking in our own corruptions as Peter was of sinking in the sea of Galilee.

Praise be to God that the Lord Jesus still responds to the cry "Lord help me", and will stretch out his hand to save. "He restoreth my soul, and leadeth me in the paths of righteousness for his own name's sake". One of the most instructive and beautiful pictures to be drawn from this story in the life of Peter is that of them walking together on those same troubled waters, Peter now hand in hand with the Lord Jesus. In those first days of love and faith I thought that for the rest of my life I would walk in the same enjoyment. To my shame I have to now say that since that time I have often left my first love, and to the praise of his amazing grace and love, the Lord has often stretched out his hand and lifted me again. When we return to him in true repentance and faith, we find that same strong and loving hand stretched out to save.

And so I in my first love, and my wife in a renewing of the love she once felt as a girl, were able to rejoice. The Holy Spirit was also pleased to renew in my wife a desire to follow the Lord in baptism, and in due time we gave our testimonies of the Lord's leadings and goodness before the church at Forest Fold. This was a great trial of faith as we were both very nervous of being asked to speak, but the Lord helped us, and we were received with much love and affection. So, at the age of 25, and in company with my wife and another friend, I was baptised by immersion in the name of the Father and of the Son and of the Holy Spirit, openly taking my place in the church of Jesus Christ on the first Sunday of November 1947.

There are two things which especially stand out in my mind about that service. The first was the preaching of the Word by our pastor. He took for his text, "I will go in the strength of the Lord God: I will make mention of thy righteousness, even of thine only" (Psalm 71 v16). This was applied to our making an open profession of faith by baptism, and what was said coincided with what was in my mind, confirming me in the step that I was taking.

The second thing was the singing of Hymn 144 in Gadsby's selection, "Jesus my all to heaven is gone." This hymn had been a great blessing to me, especially in the first verses, and I was pleased to see it had been chosen for the occasion. That day it was the last verse which moved me deeply as we sang:

Then will I tell to sinners round
What a dear Saviour I have found;
I'll point to his redeeming blood,
And say, 'Behold the way to God.'

Looking back now, as a preacher and pastor, there appears to have been something prophetic in both text and hymn. Not only were they my testimony and desire then, but they became my main objective in life, and I trust they will be till the end.

## ARISE MY LOVE

Arise my love, 'tis Jesus' voice,
  (None half so sweet beside)
Come, I have made thy soul my choice,
  And thou shalt be my bride.

Arise my love, shake off thy sleep;
  Gone is the weary night:
Come unto me, and I shall be
  Thy everlasting Light.

Arise my love, nor wonder what
  The future has at stake;
The soul that once is found in me
  I never will forsake.

Arise my love, though rough the way,
  And troubles o'er thee roll,
I am thy God, thy friend, thy stay,
  The comfort of thy soul.

Arise my love, and put thy hand
  By faith into my own;
That better than a light will be,
  If thou but trust alone.

Arise my love, and leave the toys
  That others covet so,
And I will fill thy soul with joys
  The world can never know.

## CHAPTER 4
## CALL TO THE MINISTRY

HAPPY DAYS of Christian fellowship followed, and sitting under the ministry of our beloved pastor I had no thought or desire other than to remain there a humble member all the rest of my days, and at last to be buried in the little graveyard at the back of the chapel with my forefathers.

At this stage I felt fully satisfied and fulfilled in my life. On our marriage, my wife and I moved into a spacious, newly built semi-detached house, although as yet without electric light or mains water. Situated near the top of a hill, it gave a wonderful view over the North Downs, the chalk pits near Oxted in Surrey on our left, and a panoramic view of Tunbridge Wells to the right, including the spires or towers of six of its churches. Below us lay a typical Sussex scene, with well wooded slopes and a valley through which ran a trout stream and a railway line. In the middle distance was the "Old Town" of Groombridge village, just over the border in Kent, with its famous "Walks" (a row of Tudor cottages), and the triangular green in front of them clearly visible. My parents lived next door, and my father spent many hours turning what had been the "Plum Bower" and the "Platt", two horticultural features planted by my grandfather, into gardens, rockery and rose beds.

Solomon says, "Rejoice, O young man in thy youth," and this is what I did. Although skilled in almost every branch of husbandry and farm work, much of which, like stack building, thatching, hedging, sowing corn by hand, is no longer practised, my chief concern and delight was to work with the horses. Beside the pony for pulling the trap (a two wheeled vehicle with the entrance door at the back), we normally had three farm horses. These were not massive Shires or Clydesdales, but the smaller, rather nondescript cart-horses. To get the maximum

amount of work done in a day I would take all three
out to the field, working two in a team and resting
one by turns.

From time to time horse dealers would come
round with a string of horses to sell. They would
walk from farm to farm, and then would 'put the
horses through their paces' in front of the farmer.
Occasionally my father would buy a fresh horse, or
do a deal by part exchange with one we already
possessed. The horse we had longest was a chestnut
gelding called Prince; he was an ex-army horse from
the great war (though much too young to have done
service in it). An uncle of mine can remember him
being bought by my father's brother at Lewes in
1919. "I remember that well enough" he said, "for
when William went home on the train, I had to walk
back with the horse. I couldn't ride him because he
only had a halter for leading." One to which I was
particularly attached came to us as a half-broken
colt, which I finished breaking in to farm work. He
sometimes afforded me great fun, as is evident from
the incident recorded in the following poem.

We had a fine horse, an upstanding young grey,
Who'd stood in the stable for many a day;
'Twas dead of the winter, the land was ice-bound,
A deep crisp layer of snow on the ground.

My father said, "David, it's time that we found
A job for that youngster - he's fresh, I'll be
  bound":
I said,"O,K, father, we'll make him a sleigh,
And then we can bring all the cord-wood away".

For up by the road, about half of a mile,
We'd cut down some oak trees, and made a great
  pile
Of cord-wood for firing; cold weather was here
With coal on the ration, beside being dear.

We soon made the sleigh, I'll admit it was rough,
But still, it was made of substantial stuff;
We brought out the horse - what a picture he made!-
The strength and the beauty of nature displayed.

He looked at the sleigh as he came walking by;
A glint of sly humour crept into his eye.
We hitched up the traces; he stood like a child;
We felt much relieved, but the horse merely smiled.

"Its time to get going and fetch the first lot,"
I said: at a word he was off like a shot!
"Whoa! Steady!" I said, "for there's no need to run."
But soon it was plain he was out for some fun.

For when I decided to make the next try,
He stood on two legs, with his head in the sky.
Then down went his head, and away went his heels,
He pranced up and down despite all my appeals.

I said to my work-mate, "Here, you take his head,
I'll jump on his back and will ride him instead,
And then he can gallop away at his will.
'Twill let off some steam as he runs up the hill."

I gripped with my knees, and I gathered the rein,
With one hand I got a good grip on his mane,
Then said to the laddie, "Right! let the horse go,
We're set for a gallop way over the snow."

He stood on one side and the horse gave a jump
That nigh sent me flying back over his rump;
Then up with his back-end and down with his head
To shoot me down over his withers instead.

Like a shot from a gun, or a shaft from a bow,
That little grey horse whistled over the snow;
With head in the air, and his tail straight behind,
He scarce touched the ground as he went like the wind.

The folk by the wayside stood holding their breath
To see one so foolishly courting with death;
They did not know whether to come or to go
As I thundered by in a whirlwind of snow.

At last, to my own and the others' surprise,
I brought the horse home, and was still in one piece,
But though I had conquered, I'd no room to talk -
For the rest of the week I could scarce bear to
   walk!

   In due time the Lord blessed my wife and me with two healthy children, a girl and a boy, and we looked forward to the simple, satisfying life of tilling the soil, bringing up our children, and spending the Lord's Day together in the little chapel which had been the spiritual home of both our parents and grandparents.
   God has said, "My thoughts are not your thoughts, neither are your ways my ways," and in time it became evident that the one of whom it was said, "You are Satan's chief agent among those boys," was to be the only one among them whom he had chosen to become a minister of the gospel.
   The first intimation of this came about in this way. Owing to the number of children and shortage of teachers, I was almost "press-ganged" into becoming a Sunday School teacher soon after joining the church, and was given a class of boys. It was the custom in our Sunday School to have 'Open School' once a month, when, instead of our normal classes, an address was given to the whole school. This was sometimes taken by the pastor, and at other times by male members of the Adult Bible Class or by a Sunday School teacher. Being young and inexperienced, it came as a dreadful shock to me to be told by the Sunday School superintendent, "It's your turn to take the open school next Lord's Day." No excuse would be accepted, but rather I was kindly encouraged (or admonished?) by being told, "Let no man despise thy youth."

# The Runaway Horse

The Sunday in question was Easter Sunday 1952, and I well remember sitting up late that Saturday night preparing an address on "Let your light so shine before men that they may see your good works and glorify your Father in heaven." Mr. Delves was at that time preaching on Isaiah 55, and had that day come to verse 4. "Behold, I have given him for a witness to the people, a leader and commander to the people." It was often his way of preaching to lay out the whole text with various headings and subdivisions before taking each part in greater detail, usually having the same text for all three sermons on the Sunday, and sometimes for two or even three Sundays in succession.

As I took my seat that day and bowed my head in prayer, it was as though an audible voice said, "You are to speak today of the love of Christ." To say I was startled would be an understatement: I was petrified. For one thing, I was not at that time enjoying the felt sense of the love of Christ, but rather felt totally unprepared and unqualified to take so great a subject, especially before the whole school. This is understandable as some of the Bible Class members were saints of God three nearlytimes my age. Also I was conscious of the fact that some preachers mentioned having had such an experience, and this was perhaps the most disturbing element of all. My mind was in a turmoil throughout the whole sermon, but in outlining the last clause, "a commander to the people", Mr. Delves spoke briefly of "Following him in love". Through that the Lord was pleased to renew a feeling of love to the Lord Jesus in my heart, and I resolved to speak from Peter's words in John 21 v17, "Lord, thou knowest all things; thou knowest that I love thee."

Although there had been little time for preparation, as I began to speak all nervousness was taken from me, the Lord opened the word up to my mind, and I was able to speak freely and feelingly. I knew enough of my own sinful heart and failure in

Forest Fold Baptist Chapel, Crowborough.

Originally a barn, it is now a typical country chapel and congregation. My parents were baptised here by Mr. E. Littleton, who was pastor for 52 years, and my wife and I by Mr. S. Delves who followed him, and was pastor for the next 53.

life to be able to identify with Peter, and say as Asaph, "my heart was grieved, and I was pricked in my reins. So foolish was I, and ignorant: I was as a beast before thee." I knew also enough of the love of God shed abroad in my heart at that moment to be able to share with others something of his love to me, and the response of love awakened in my own heart. I remember quoting with fresh understanding and feeling the words of a hymn we sometimes sang:
> If all the trees were counted o'er,
> And all the sand upon the shore,
> With every drop of rain that fell
> No numbers Jesus' love can tell.

Another custom observed at Forest Fold was that instead of a preaching service in the afternoon on first Sundays, the whole time was taken up by the observance of the Lord's Supper. As we sat quietly waiting for the service to begin, the voice spoke again: simple, short and unmistakable in meaning: "Follow me." This was a call, not to feed the lambs in the Sunday School, but sheep in the wider fields of ministry. I sat and trembled as the implications of such a call came forcibly to me, and I thought of others, older, more able and gracious men in the church, who I knew were exercised about the ministry. Like Peter I said in my mind "What of them?" Again the words of Jesus came vividly to my mind, "What is that to thee? Follow thou me."

This made such a deep impression upon me that I related all these things to my pastor that same day. In doing so I not only acknowledged my lack of ability and grace, and the experience necessary for so high a calling, but my positive unwillingness to take it up. He wisely counselled me to watch, wait and pray, believing the Lord would reveal his will more fully if it was to be. He had a great fear of men running "Unsent" with no clear message, as in the case of Ahimaaz (2 Samuel 18; v22, 29). When asked what news he brought concerning the king's son he could only say, "I saw a great tumult, but I did not know what it was about."

The Lord graciously dealt with my unwillingness before I went to bed that night, by giving me the promise, "Thy people shall be willing in the day of thy power." Although feeling my lack of education or natural ability, I knew there was no real reason why God could not use me if he so purposed. There were many men of former generations who could scarcely read or write, and yet they were men of God, filled with the Spirit, and greatly used in the extension of Christ's kingdom.

Many a time have I thought of an old, bearded, illiterate man who preached his first sermon in Smart's Hill chapel when I was still quite young. My parents had worshipped in this chapel when they were first married, and we returned there for one Sunday a year all my boyhood days. This minister said he could not preach from a text, only give a "running commentary" on a passage of scripture – much to the delight of my brother Joe, who made a joke about a football match, or horse racing. The old man was speaking about Jesus before Pilate, and I remember him saying, "They accused him vehemently, friends. Vehemently they did – whatever that means; I dunno meself, I baint very learned about such things." This was also a cause of merriment to some, but as he had been talking simply about the sufferings of the Lord Jesus Christ, something had touched my young heart. I remember bowing my head below the plain wooden pew, and praying for the old man a prayer I had so often heard prayed for our pastor and other ministering brethren at Forest Fold: "Lord, give him seals to his ministry, and souls for his hire." I was far too young to know what that prayer meant, but as I believe the poor man was never again asked there to preach, I wonder whether, when he appears before the Master, he will find that the only seal to his ministry, the only soul for his hire, was the little ploughboy who bowed his head in Smart's Hill chapel that day. Who knows? for none can tell that secret moment when a soul is quickened into life by the Spirit of God.

The Interior of Smarts Hill Chapel
I was taken to this typical Kent wood-framed chapel as a babe: preached from this pulpit when a man.

## CHAPTER 5
## IMMERSION IN THE SPIRIT

THERE HAD been times when preachers, relating some experience of their call to the ministry, had spoken in my hearing of having to "tarry until endued with power from on high". Thus began a diligent search on my part to discover how I, as "unlearned and ignorant" as Peter was, weak, sinful, and utterly inadequate in myself, could be endued with power as a true minister of the gospel should be.

Some men I knew personally had been exercised for many years concerning the ministry, and were waiting on the Lord for such an experience or word as would enable them to go forth with confidence; others I read about had waited half a life-time. It was three years from the time the Lord first called Peter, "Follow me," to the time when he was baptised with the Spirit and received the fulfilment of the promise to be endued with power.

Although absolutely convinced the Lord had called me to preach the gospel, I was equally convinced that I could not, should not, and would not, attempt to do so unless and until I knew "the day of his power". These two convictions presented me with a problem. What did I need to transform me from a <u>believer in</u> the gospel to a <u>preacher of</u> the gospel?

It was then I began seriously to consider what it was to be baptised with the Holy Ghost. This was a subject which I had never, to my knowledge, heard mentioned from the pulpit. I possessed no theological or study books, neither had I any knowledge of the Pentecostal church and teaching. I entered into this study with no preconceived ideas, and no books other than my Bible, a good concordance, and an English dictionary, but I believed the promise Jesus had given concerning the Holy Spirit, "He shall lead you into all truth". As a Baptist, I had no difficulty in knowing what the word "baptise" really meant, and one copy of the Bible I possessed (Gender's Revision of the Authorised), actually used the word "immerse" for the Greek words variously translated baptise, baptism etc. in our English Bible. An explanatory note about this stated that the word baptise was simply the transference of the Greek sound to the English language, not a true translation, but what is known as transliteration. I concluded that if to be baptised with water meant to be immersed, then I must accept the same meaning of the word when used of the Spirit, as it is actually rendered in Gender's version.

That one could be a true believer, possessing the Spirit of Christ, and yet not truly immersed in his Spirit, I felt to be true of myself, and of many others. I remember an old uncle of mine telling me of a deacon he had known, of whom he said, "He was a cantankerous old man, quite impossible to live with - but you should have heard him in prayer: he was wonderful in prayer." I thought then, and have often thought since, that his family would have rather he had been a little less wonderful in prayer, and more Christ-like to live with.

> O the Spirit-filled life; is it thine? is it thine?
> Is thy soul wholly filled with the Spirit Divine?
> O thou child of the King, has he fallen on thee?
> Does he reign in thy soul so that all men may see
> The dear Saviour's image reflected in thee?

Acts chapter 8 especially held my attention. It became apparent to me that in Samaria there were true believers, born of the Spirit, who in some way had not been baptised (or immersed) with the Spirit, for "as yet he had fallen upon none of them". It was only as the apostles laid hands on them that they experienced the same blessing as the apostles on the day of Pentecost.

Further to this, I discovered that Timothy received the gift of God through the laying on of Paul's hands, even as Paul himself was filled with the Holy Ghost through the ministry of Ananias. It was only after Paul had baptised the disciples at Ephesus (having satisfied himself they had become true believers in the Lord Jesus), that he laid hands on them, and the Holy Spirit "came upon them". Paul also gave instruction in this matter with regard to those whom Timothy would be instrumental in sending into the ministry.

Just prior to this, I had been introduced to a godly bishop in the Free Church of England, and being resolved to leave no stone unturned in seeking such an experience, I resolved to go and ask him to lay hands on me. Other business took me to the area where he lived, and so I went to see him. We talked together for a considerable time, and I told him of my felt spiritual poverty and need. As we talked, I became aware of the fact that there was no need for me to ask for the laying on of hands, though I felt sure he would have done so had I asked.

For one thing, I considered it might be improper for me to go to a man of a different Denomination for this; my own pastor was the one to whom I ought to go. Yet I doubted if he would have done so, or if I had faith to believe it would be of benefit. Of even greater importance was the realisation that everything we receive, we receive by faith according to his Word. While I believe that the laying on of hands is a scriptural means of grace, albeit neglected by some and abused by others, yet the promise is, "How much more will your heavenly Father give the Holy Spirit to them that ask him," Also we read in Galatians that we receive the promise of the Spirit through faith. Although the reference there is speaking specifically of the gift of the Spirit received initially at the time of regeneration, it was this scripture which came to my mind as I talked to the bishop, and convinced me that I must turn from any man or means, and wait solely upon the Lord.

There is much I would like to say on this subject, as it has, through all the years of my ministry, appeared to me a very important one. Suffice it now to say that I do not hold to the Pentecostal view that the "Baptism of the Spirit" is a second stage in the life of a believer which thereafter maintains him on a higher plane of spiritual life. Nor that 'speaking in tongues' as it is normally practised today is an evidence of being baptised with the Holy Spirit. Neither do I hold the view that the term "Baptism of the Spirit" should be confined exclusively to initiation into the Christian life, as advocated by modern Evangelical theologians. I have dear, beloved brethren in Christ who hold to one or the other of these opposing theological conceptions, but I have read or observed nothing which has altered two further convictions which came to me as I studied and prayed over this subject at that time.

First, that when the Lord Jesus said to his disciples, "You shall be baptised with the Holy Spirit not many days from now"(Acts 1 v5), he was not speaking of something which is automatically true of every believer when he or she is "baptised by the Spirit into the body of Christ" (1 Corinthians 12 v13, where the body of Christ is clearly the church, as taught in that chapter and stated elsewhere). While every believer receives the Spirit in regeneration, and Pentecost was a unique occasion in which the New Testament church once and for all received the Spirit to abide until Christ returns, I believe there is also for the believer a personal experience of being baptised (immersed) with the Spirit. Many believers have had an experience which could be described as such, and what could better describe those blessed seasons of revival with which God has from time to time blessed his people, than to use the same terms as used of Pentecost, saying, 'He poured out his

Spirit,' or, 'The Holy Ghost fell on them'? Peter says of the house of Cornelius, "As I began to speak, the Holy Ghost fell on them, as on us at the beginning. Then remembered I the word of the Lord, how he said, 'John indeed baptised with water; but ye shall be baptised with the Holy Ghost... God gave to them the like gift as he did unto us who believed on the Lord Jesus Christ'."

At that time I knew nothing of either Doctor Martyn Lloyd Jones or Duncan Campbell, two men greatly used of God this century, who saw true Holy Spirit revival brought about through their ministry here in the United Kingdom. These men, in some respects so different, both held there was a difference between being born of the Spirit, and being baptised with the Spirit. To quote Duncan Campbell: "There is nothing on earth so deadening as truth preached without the anointing of God, without the Holy Ghost. Orthodox preaching without heaven's anointing. Personally I see no hope for the church unless there is a re-disovery of the truth, and men acting upon it,'Ye shall receive power after that the Holy Ghost is come you; and ye shall be witnesses to me'". What I did know was that I needed the anointing of the Holy Spirit, power from on high, before I could be an effective preacher of the gospel.

Secondly, I came to feel that the Lord had in fact already given me such an experience, and that I may have grieved him by not responding to his command, "Follow me." I resolved that if he would renew such a time of knowing what it was to be immersed in his love, conscious of my whole being coming under the gracious influence and power of the Holy Spirit, I would now obey without any hesitation. I continued therefore to watch, wait and pray, but it was not until 1955 that the Lord was pleased to answer my request and give me the confirmation I needed to go forward.

Lamberhurst Chapel, Kent.

The baptising pool in this chapel was kept full by rainwater from the roof. One Sunday I preached here from the text, "The time to favour Zion is come". On entering the pulpit I saw a fresh family present. The man was Jabez Field, who later became pastor.

## CHAPTER 6
## A MINISTER OF THE GOSPEL

ABOUT A year after I had felt the Lord calling me into the work of the gospel ministry, my father decided to retire from work, and hand over to me the responsibility of managing our small farm. He did not, as I had anticipated and indeed had been promised, simply hand it over to me, although I had now worked for him for nearly twenty years on a very low wage. Instead, he decided to form a limited company. I believe one reason for this was to safeguard legally my elder brother, whose health by this time had greatly deteriorated. My father was not at that time aware of my exercise regarding the ministry, as it was the custom among our churches not to disclose any such leadings to anyone but the pastor. The fact that I was the only worker out of five directors (my parents, my brother, a sister in America, and myself) meant that I had responsibilities difficult to lay down when I later became a pastor.

However, I was happy with the situation at that time, and began with great enthusiasm to set about implementing some of my own ideas for improving the business, which up until then had mainly been producing market garden crops for sale to local retailers. The main ingredient of this new enterprise was a plan to build up a small herd of pedigree Guernsey cows, and after the old cowshed had been modernised, the foundation stock was bought at a farm sale near Haywards Heath. They proved to be a good investment, and I came to love these beautiful creatures with their rich yellow milk and quiet ways - "Golden Guernseys" they were in more ways than one.

Although I threw myself wholeheartedly into the new project, experimenting with new varieties of fruit, and thoroughly reorganising the business, the exercise of the ministry was constantly upon my mind. My pastor was a cautious man with regard to sending men into the ministry, and fearful of over-encouraging them. He believed it was best to leave such matters entirely to the leading of the Spirit in the life of the individual concerned. During the three years that elapsed between my 'first' and 'second' call, he only ever mentioned the subject once, and that was simply to say, "David, I have not forgotten what you disclosed to me about your feelings toward the ministry, and I continue to watch, wait and pray."

I use the term 'first' and 'second' call, as I perceive in my own experience what we see in the history of Peter, as recorded in the Gospels. He received a call by the side of Lake Galilee, "Follow me, and I will make you a fisher of men." Approximately three and a quarter years later, that call was repeated, as is recorded in John 21 v19, 22: "Follow me." It is remarkable that in the providence of God it was three and a quarter years after I first heard these words, as I sat waiting at the Lord's Table in Forest Fold chapel, that the call was renewed.

In the spring of 1955 I had to take to bed with extreme physical and mental prostration. This was something new to me, as I had always enjoyed good health and unbounding energy. My pastor came to see me, and realising that the physical weakness was linked with spiritual conflict, said, "David, if your exercise about the ministry has brought you to this, I think it is time to share the matter with the church."

To the doctor who came to examine me I said, "Doctor, I don't think there is anything physically wrong with me." He was one of the old school who never discussed things with his patients, or normally gave anything away, but as he left the room he said, "I think your diagnosis is correct. You must get right away and see what a few days change will do." So within a day or two I went to Sompting, where an uncle and aunt lived who worshipped at Broadwater Baptist Church. The first night I was there, the Sunday School had their anniversary and I went to it with them, little expecting what the Lord was preparing for me.

The speaker at that time was talking to the children about Moses, and how the Lord met with him in the back side of the desert, forty years after he had failed in an attempt to do what he evidently thought was God's will for him, by seeking to ease the burden of his brethren under the Egyptian slave masters. The text was Exodus 4 v2, "And the Lord said unto him, 'What is in thy hand?' And he said, 'A rod'" - only a dried stick, is how the preacher described it. As the man on the platform directed his words to the children, and demonstrated what the Lord had enabled Moses to do with that dried stick, the Lord directed the message to my heart. I felt revived and encouraged that God could and would take me and my 'dried stick' to be of some use in his service.

That night my mind went back over the message I had heard, and realised that the objections Moses had made were so much like my own. I was particularly concerned about my lack of education and ability to speak. As I lay in bed the Lord was pleased once more to visit my soul with a sense of his love, grace, and all-sufficiency. My spirit, and indeed my whole being, revived under the gracious ministry of the Spirit, and when the words that God had spoken to Moses, "Now, therefore go, and I will be with thy mouth and teach thee what thou shalt say" were spoken into my heart with divine power, I remember saying, "Thank you, Lord; I will write to Mr. Delves tomorrow." With that a great sense of relief and peace came over me, and I turned over in bed and went to sleep in a way I had not been able to do for months.

In many of our Strict Baptist churches it has been the custom for any man who felt called to preach, to do so before the church members as part of the procedure for 'sending him forth into the ministry . My pastor was not in favour of this 'preaching a trial sermon', as he called it, believing it was better to seek to discern the Lord's will in the matter, together with the scriptural requirements for an elder and the observance of the necessary gifts being present. Then, when the church had heard and approved of his testimony regarding his personal exercise and calling, that the brother concerned be invited to preach at a normal Sunday service before being recommended to other churches. This procedure was followed in my case, and in due time I came before the church, and was accepted.

I preached my first sermon on the last Sunday afternoon in July 1955. When that day came, I and many others were amazed at the clarity of speech given to one who was by nature, as Moses expressed, slow of speech and of a slow tongue. To this day I am conscious that the liberty of speech, and command of language which are usually present in my preaching, are due only to the fulfilment of that promise. Often have I prayed with David, "Lord, remember the word, unto thy servant, on which thou hast caused me to hope." He has not failed me, nor forsaken me, and to him alone be the glory.

No doubt every minister can remember the text from which he first preached. With me, it was Ephesians 3 v8: "Unto me, who am less than the least of all saints, is this grace given, that I should preach among the Gentiles the unsearchable riches of Christ." Throughout the years I have sought to make this theme central to my ministry, but over recent years have realised this was only one part of a twofold commission given to the apostle Paul. He goes on to say. "and to make all men see what is the fellowship of the mystery, which from the beginning of the world hath been hid in God" - that mystery being the unity of all true believers. "That the Gentiles should be fellow heirs, of the same body, and partakers of his promise in Christ through the gospel" (vv. 3-6). If we become one with Christ, we ought to see we are one with all who are in Christ, and as we consider the teaching of the apostle Paul, we see the great doctrine of the unity of the body of Christ constantly brought forward.

As soon as it became certain that I was about to enter into the gospel ministry, it also became apparent that there would need to be changes in the business. My father was particularly concerned that the pressure of market gardening, which included finding suitable outlets for very perishable produce, and the possibility of my being called to be the pastor of a church, would necessitate folding up the business, and even perhaps selling up the family home and moving elsewhere.

Cowper says, "God moves in a mysterious way his wonders to perform," and this is a truth I have often seen demonstrated. So it was, that as soon as I responded to the call to go at the Lord's command, a gentleman tenant farmer who had taken a small farm adjacent to our own and rented large tracts of land on Buckhurst estate, died suddenly in the midst of life. This man had invested in modern buildings, which on the few acres belonging to the farm itself, made the holding over-capitalised and useless as a single unit. When it came on the market to rent, it was just what I needed to house my expanding herd and move from intensive market gardening to the more easily managed mixed farm, where we would be able to extend the herd to forty head of milking cows.

Many people have wondered how it is possible for a working farmer, who works long days, and has a longer working wèek than almost any other calling, to also be a minister or pastor, but I have never found this to be a problem. Partly this may be because of the mental attitude of the small farmer, who, although dedicated to his work and stock, takes an objective view of the numerous problems and the losses that are inevitably his lot. Although the Bible teaches that the preacher must not be 'entangled' with the things of this life it does not forbid being engaged in them. Paul, who has been singled out as the example we should follow (Phil.3 v17, & 4 v9;), laboured with his own hands in order not to be a financial burden to the church.

    I remember reading about a pastor who was at first delighted to have a cow of his own, but after a short time had to part with it saying, "My cow followed me into the pulpit", meaning it came between him and his ministry. In contrast to this, I well remember one cow was missing on a Sunday morning, and being particularly concerned about it because there was a ban on cattle movement, due to an outbreak of Foot and Mouth disease. After a fruitless search which lasted until the time I had to leave for my preaching engagement, and after committing it to the Lord in prayer, the matter was completely removed from my mind. It was not until I was on my homeward journey that evening that I gave it another thought. I learned next morning that the cow had been found safe, deep in a wood on an adjoining estate. Although the hymn is a modern one, the godly farmer has, perhaps above many, always been conscious of the principle expressed:

    Father I place into your hands
    The things I cannot do;
    Father I place into your hands
    The things that I've been through;
    Father I place into your hands
    The way that I should go,
    For I know I always can trust you.

    The rented farm included a good farmhouse into which a dear brother christian who had come to work for us could move. His faithful service, and the new set-up, freed me to devote the time needed to maintain an itinerant ministry. The additional buildings and facilities also gave a boost to another ministry which my wife and I had initiated - that of bringing together the children and young people from a number of Sunday Schools and Chapels for a day's fellowship and games on the farm. Those gatherings were nostalgic for those who had been used to pre-war "Sunday School treats", and were greatly enjoyed by all. Although no attempt was made at that time to bring a gospel message, there was spiritual benefit derived as well as healthy exercise, and last but perhaps not least, a number of young people met suitable partners who later married and formed Christian families.

The circle of ministers and type of ministry into which I entered at the age of 33 is one which is fast disappearing in all but a small part of the Christian Church in England today. My pastor's regular ministry was the only tuition I had for the ministry, and somehow I thought there were three golden rules for preaching:

1. have something worth saying, and say it so that the people could hear and understand.
2. never use notes.
3. preach for at least forty-five minutes.

This may sound ridiculous now, but I am sure that if - and in some cases perhaps only if - a man fulfilled those three rules, he would have been regarded as a good preacher.

There are many advantages to be gained from higher education, Bible College training, and the wealth of Christian literature, both from the old divines and present day theologians, of which today's preacher can avail himself. There are also some disadvantages, particularly in the fact that a man may preach a good sermon with the power of another man's words and a gift of eloquence, but without that indefinable element which was so often present in the preaching of simple men of bygone days - 'the unction of the Spirit'. Most of the great preachers of the past had both education and the Spirit. I often ask myself, do we? Instead of being "men of the Book", are we becoming "men of the books"? We do not want a return to that form of experimental preaching, once prevalent in some circles, which constantly turned the attention of the hearers inward to their feelings, but it is important that the preacher should have a word from the Lord to convey to the people, and not simply a sound theological or practical exposition of some passage of Scripture. How often the cry of the preacher, as the hour of preaching approached, was, "Lord, I haven't got a text. I don't know what message Thou hast for the people." Still today this exercise is with me, though now with a humble confidence in a faithful God who never fails those who put their trust in him. The cry, however, still haunts me in my dreams, usually in the form of being in the pulpit, opening the Bible where I think the text should be, and finding unfamiliar words, sometimes not even the scripture. Perhaps this goes back to the very first occasion on which I went out to preach.

On my first Sunday preaching engagement away from my home church, in a little chapel in the village of Lamberhurst, the Lord graciously gave me a text and considerable prior meditation on the subject. He enabled me to fulfil the first two of these rules, but the forty-five minutes swallowed up both morning and afternoon sermons! At that chapel the minister was expected to bring his own food for dinner. As I sat eating my sandwiches during the hour and a half between the services, I said to the deacon, "I don't know what I am going to preach about this afternoon." To my surprise he did not seem the least disturbed or concerned about that, and years later, when a very old man, would refer to that comment and tell of the blessing he had received that day.

Indeed, the Lord was very gracious to me, for though I must have looked as miserable as I felt, an old lady present came and preached me a sermon that showed how wrong my supposed third rule was. She gently touched me on the shoulder saying kindly,

"Cheer up, despondent saint, and trust in Jesus' blood." A nine word sermon which has helped me through many times of distress and temptation ever since.

That afternoon I preached from Psalm 34 v15: "The eyes of the Lord are upon the righteous, and his ears are open to their cry". I was conscious of the Lord fulfilling that promise, even as I preached, and in contrast to the morning, the forty-five minutes seemed to speed away.

The line of the hymn quoted by this dear saint, who was old enough to be my grandmother, and wise enough to be my teacher, may not have been inspired as is the scripture, but it is "something worth saying" and I want to repeat it so that all may "hear and understand":

CHEER UP, DESPONDENT SAINT, AND TRUST IN JESUS' BLOOD.

Another incident of a very different nature comes to mind as I think of those early years. It was my first visit to a large chapel and congregation in London, and I was to be met at the railway station by a deacon who would escort me to the chapel. As I came up to the gate at the end of the platform I could see him standing there and anxiously scanning the passengers for the new minister. Dressed immaculately in black jacket and pin-striped trousers, wearing the customary black bowler, he did not even look at the young man who came through the turnstile wearing a plain gaberdine riding mac, and with a mass of curly hair overtopping a sunburnt face. I quietly waited by his side, and when the last passenger passed through, he turned aside disappointedly until I spoke his name. To the dear man's credit he never raised an eyebrow at my unorthodox appearance, but received me cordially, and became a dear friend and an appreciative hearer.

Having to milk the cows before going out to preach on a Sunday meant most of my engagements were in the local country chapels. Yet it was not only for that reason that I (unless feeling some special leading from the Lord), confined my own ministry to the area in which I lived. To me it seemed inappropriate for men to travel great distances, often spending the whole weekend away from wife and family, while local churches were also engaging ministers from a distance, perhaps from the very area to which one of their own members had gone to preach.

Those little country chapels! What tales could be told of dear souls and quaint ways! The custom of reading the whole hymn verse by verse before it was sung without any musical accompaniment still prevailed in some places. The original purpose for this was because few people could read. As more of the population became able to do so, and hymnbooks came into common use, the practice began to die out. Where it was retained, and the verses read prayerfully and intelligently, it would no doubt have fixed the words more firmly in the people's minds. It is surprising how many hymns some of these older folk knew by heart. I was amazed the first time that I encountered this, as the deacon reading the hymn did so in a very high, almost falsetto, voice, and then dropped into a deep bass voice when it came to singing, taking two or three breaths for every line because the singing was so slow. No one in the congregation saw anything unusual in this procedure, although it seemed so strange to me. There was a further surprise at the end, for they sang the last hymn without reading each verse, and considerably faster than the other two!

Some of the chapels were still lit by oil lamps, and one to which I went had an aladdin lamp close to the pulpit. At the close of the reading I saw a man in the congregation looking anxiously at this lamp, and turning my own gaze towards it I noticed a little black patch beginning to form on the mantle. I can see now the look of surprise and pleasure on his face, and the little nod of approval I was given, as I gently turned down the wick in the correct way to clear away the patch.

There was the little chapel at Barcombe, so small, with a pulpit so low and near the reading desk, that when I realised the old deacon, who was rather deaf, had not heard what chapter had been given out, I was able to bend over the pulpit and find the place for him. The welcome I received there, and the love shown to me over many years, has made that spot very precious, although, through the goodness of God, the old chapel became too small, and a new building has been erected by its side.

I recall the old lady at East Hoathly, who complained loudly that she could not hear the sermon. "I can't hear him", she 'whispered' to her her sister. "Have you got your hearing aid on?" this good soul inquired in an equally loud whisper. "No" came the reply, "I heard he was supposed to have a good voice, so I haven't brought it with me. I thought it would be a treat". And that was in a building with the worst acoustics I have ever encountered. That chapel has long since closed, and reverted to its original purpose as a dwelling place.

There used to be a saying, "as poor as a church mouse", but I can affirm that country chapel mice are fat and flourishing. They could be a menace to the preacher, for when the mouse came out of his hole, all concentration and profit went out of the window, or at least out of the preaching. It wasn't only the youngsters who would be looking and wondering where it would pop up next: I well remember chasing a mouse out of the upstairs Sunday School where it was distracting the attention of the children I was addressing, only to have it turn up in the chapel in the middle of the afternoon sermon, just when I felt to have the full attention of the congregation. It had the audacity to come out to the front, stand up on its hind legs, and peer up at me in the pulpit as if it recognised my voice, then it wrinkled its nose in defiance and ran right over the foot of the young lady organist. She retained great composure, but the boys in the back were all agog watching its progress, and even father could not suppress a smile or two. When it comes to competing with a mouse for attention the preacher will often find himself on the losing side.

In some country districts where there are morning and afternoon services, the whole congregation might go to another little chapel in the evening to "keep the doors open" in anticipation of the Lord sending revival. I remember one such occasion in Mayford, when the folk from Knaphill intended to celebrate the Lord's Supper with a few other local believers who attended that chapel. As I was waiting in the minister's vestry, one of the deacons came in to inform me that his fellow deacon had returned to his house to get the bread, which had been forgotten. The reason for this brother's absence was mentioned at the beginning of the service, and before attempting to read the scripture that evening, for my own peace of mind I had to tell the congregation that the text from which I intended to preach was "Why reason ye among yourselves, (is it) because ye have brought no bread?" (Matthew 16 v8).

It has been my privilege to minister in a wide variety of churches and chapels, but wherever I have gone I have found some who loved the Lord and His word enough to overlook our differences because of the common bond we have in Christ. I call to mind preaching to a large well-to-do upper middle class congregation on the woman of the city who came to Jesus in the house of Simon the pharisee, and challenging them clearly with the question, "Would this woman be welcome here?" Much to my comfort and delight the senior deacon came to me after the service and said, "I'm so glad you said what you did about that poor woman: there are a lot of people in this church who only want 'respectable sinners' here." That day there was a bond formed between us as between Jonathan and David, and although the age-gap between us was great, it continued until the day of his death.

Many years ago I had an interesting conversation with a young Jamaican as we stood in the shadow of the great stones of Stonehenge, and have never forgotten one remark he made. He said, "My father taught me never to judge a nation or a denomination by the action of individuals." I have found this true also of churches. On hearing that I had been asked to preach at a certain chapel one of the older members of our church said, "You going there! They ought to have the word PRIDE written in 3ft. letters across the front of that chapel." What I found was something quite different, for although there were some wealthy people there, and they were a little more exclusive than I had been used to, I was received with kindness and love, and my ministry was appreciated among them.

At the other end of the scale, when preaching in a small mission hall type of building one of the leading members said to me, "You are a Baptist, but not a <u>Strict</u> Baptist are you?" When I replied in the affirmative, this was followed by a second question, "But not a Strict and <u>Particular</u> Baptist, surely?" Being given the opportunity to explain what that meant to the company I did so, explaining the term "Particular" by saying, "I have a love for all children, but a particular love for my own. God has a love to all his creatures, for he so loved the world as to give his only begotten Son, but he has a particular love for his own children, chosen in Christ." This admittedly is a little short in theology, but through the illustration the message went home. These people also loved the Lord Jesus Christ, and our love to one another in Him overcame the considerable difference between my Calvinistic and their Arminian approach, so that I preached the gospel of God's grace there a number of times.

Among the local chapels in which I preached before becoming a pastor was one at Scaynes Hill. On my first visit I preached on the parable of the drag net (Matthew 13 v47). The solemnity of that message, together with a sense of urgency which gripped my soul as I preached upon the good being gathered into vessels and the bad being cast away, comes vividly to my mind as I recall the occasion. Nearly thirty years later I was told by one present of the deep impression made upon her that day by the word of God. This is not the only instance of hearing in recent years of blessing which attended those early years of ministry, and has caused my heart to melt under the goodness of God. He will ever fulfil his promise, "He that goeth forth and weepeth, bearing precious seed, shall doubtless come again with rejoicing, bringing his sheaves with him." To other fellow labourers who may at times be tempted to feel they have "run in vain, and spent their strength for nought" I would say with the apostle, "My beloved brethren, be ye steadfast, unmoveable, always abounding in the work of the Lord, knowing that your labour is not in vain in the Lord."

The first long journey I ever undertook in preaching the word was 140 miles to Chippenham, Wiltshire, in January 1956. This was a great exercise to me, and it was also to the deacon who made the engagement, for he had only just undertaken that duty, and I was the first minister he had engaged as a "new man". Here again spiritual bonds were formed which time and change have not affected, save only to deepen and enrich. I remember preaching in those early days there from "My soul thirsteth for God, for the living God", and later asking one of the lads who were present, "Does your soul thirst for God?" Never shall I forget the heartfelt way in which he replied, "Ah! it does that!" He had evidently been seeking the Lord, and although not brought into liberty through my preaching, I rejoiced when the Lord fulfilled for him the promise, "They that seek shall find."

It was also there at Chippenham that I first saw the Lord's hand at work in granting immediate physical healing. I knew this dear brother was very ill, and as I arrived on the doorstep one Saturday night, met a local pastor who had been to visit him. As this man turned to leave he said to my friend's wife, "I believe John is ready to go", and it quickly became apparent to me that things were much more serious than I thought, his life was believed to hang in the balance. After a while I went up to his bedroom, and when I opened my Bible at the book of James chapter 5, the words, "the prayer of faith shall heal the sick", riveted my attention. At that moment I was filled with an assurance that God would raise this brother up from his sick bed, and closing the Bible I knelt beside the bed and prayed with God given faith that the Lord would heal.

In the morning his wife surprised me by saying, "David, John says he is going to get up and go to chapel", and then in a tone of wonder and awe asked, "Is it a miracle?" Although I had felt quite confident that the Lord would heal, I had anticipated that there would possibly be some weeks before real improvement, but it soon became apparent that it was indeed a miracle of divine healing. The littleness of my faith could hardly grasp the reality of what had taken place, and proved again the truth contained in the hymn: "Prayer is appointed to convey the blessings God <u>designs to give.</u>"

When referring to this incident in 1990, I discovered that what John most remembered was the word the Lord had given me to preach from that day, "Where sin abounded, grace did much more abound." He spoke particularly of an illustration I used in explaining the text to the younger members

Caterham Chapel, Surrey.

Fifty years ago this church was on the point of extinction. Now the corrugated iron structure has been replaced with a much better building, and the church has prospered. The Austen Seven belonged to a deacon who was largely responsible for this change of the congregation, of how my children and I had built a great sand castle, with strong walls to keep the sea out as long as possible, but the sea had come in and abounded over it all. When the tide turned and went out the sand was once again smooth and level, not a vestige of the castle was left, and so had grace abounded where sin had once reigned. The fact that God had healed his sin-weary soul was evidently a greater miracle to this dear child of God than the physical healing of the body.

"How good is the God we adore,
Our faithful unchangeable friend,
His love is as great as his power,
And knows neither measure nor end."

One more "first" which must be mentioned was my first baptismal service, which took place at Caterham. Having been twice swept out of my depth when bathing in the sea, I had a fear of water, and on being asked to baptise someone who had been blessed through my ministry, I begged hard for someone else actually to baptise this person following my preaching the sermon. But no excuse would be accepted, and with great trepidation I began to step down into the water. The moment I did so, a surge of strength swept over me, commencing at my ankles, and passing right up through my body. What began in fear and trembling was accomplished with ease and great joy. The confidence given at that time has never been lost, and I believe the Lord has been pleased to impart it to many that I have since baptised, even those who at first were as fearful as I had been. To him be the glory!

Looking back over those years, I thank God for the many dear, gracious people who received me into their homes and hearts, who encouraged me in my ministry, and often enriched my soul with their counsel and conversation. Many a time did the Lord minister to my own soul through his Holy Spirit as I endeavoured to minister to his people. Deep and lifelong friendships were formed as the Lord was felt to be among us, blessing his word to both young and old. There is no need for me to record the names of the various chapels at which I preached, or try and recall the many tokens I had of the Lord blessing the word spoken. It is sufficient to say that he was better to me than all my fears, and faithful to his word of promise.

After twelve months in which I relied on public transport, or on borrowing a motorcycle and side car from a cousin, the Lord made it possible for me to buy a little 1938 Morris 8, series E, which gave me several years of good service before being passed on to a fellow member, Mr. Henry Godley, who had also been called into the ministry. Sometimes I would come home singing the doxology because the Lord had blessed us, and at other times returning with a heavy heart and sense of shame that I had failed to fulfil my high calling. On one occasion, as I walked from the car to the house feeling such an utter failure that I wondered how I would ever be able to preach again, it was as though the Lord spoke audibly, "Let us hold fast the profession of our faith without wavering, for he is faithful that promised." My spirits revived as I realised that my sins and failures did not in any way alter the faithfulness of God to his promise, and so by his grace and enabling I continued.

## CHAPTER 7
## VISION? OR DREAM?

BEFORE CONTINUING with the main purpose of recording the events and experiences which changed me from a ploughboy to a pastor, I would like to record something else I believe the Lord showed me when, in 1954, I was earnestly seeking his enabling power and grace to obey the Saviour's command to "follow me."

When studying and praying over Ezekiel 37, and seeking its fulfilment in my own soul, I was given a strong persuasion that not only would the Lord send revival to me, but that, if I lived to the average age of my forebears - about 82 years - I would also see revival on a worldwide scale such as has never been witnessed before.

It came to me in this way; that as bone came to bone, so there would be a revival of interest in the doctrines of grace, which are surely the framework of the true church, but this would not bring revival itself. Also, as the sinews and flesh came upon them, so there would follow a revival of true biblical order and experimental spiritual life, but neither would these things bring revival. Following this there would be a mighty movement of the Holy Spirit, the breath of God, and the church would be raised from its lifeless state to that of an exceeding great army.

When this persuasion came to me there was presented to my mind the figure of twenty year periods; twenty years for the bones to come together; twenty years during which Bible-based churches of born-again believers would be established on a worldwide scale; and some time during the next twenty years (i.e. from 1994 onwards) a mighty outpouring of the Holy Spirit. I can give no reason for these twenty year periods other than to repeat that they were presented to my mind at that time. As I knew that Strict Baptists held the doctrines of grace, kept close to New Testament church order, required an experimental knowledge of the truth, and were insistent on the fact that "we need a Holy Ghost religion", I believed revival would come among our own churches. When I shared this with my own pastor, he made two comments which have remained clearly in my mind.

(1) I was not the only young man who believed in and hoped to see revival, and he was therefore encouraged that it would come. "But" he said, "Not in my day, My generation will mainly experience a general decline, and that is for the most part all we can see. If the Lord is giving younger men a vision for revival, then there is good reason to believe that they will live to see it."

(2) In his view of church history, denominations had often sprung out of God-sent revival, but seldom if ever had God-sent revival sprung out of a denomination.

He was greatly concerned for the future of Strict Baptists <u>as a denomination,</u> and before I left he asked me to pray. Oh, how I poured out my heart to God that he would renew his work in me. That he would give to all his believing people such an experience of his love, power and presence as he had graciously granted to me, and that he would pour out his Spirit upon the church. That he would send revival, such as had been experienced in certain times and locations, but in a greater and world-wide way!

Being himself greatly moved Mr. Delves said, "David, if the Lord is pleased to answer your prayer, it will be like putting new wine into an old wineskin - our old denominational bottle will perish." With great warmth of feeling I replied, "That would not matter, so that the church of God is blessed." To this he made no reply, but quietly and thoughtfully smiled in his characteristic way. Looking back over my experience as a pastor, I wonder whether he was thinking of the rest of that saying,"...and the wine will be lost."

Now, nearly forty years later, I see that a renewed interest in the doctrines of grace, which are now known as the Reformed Faith, has taken place among the churches, largely through books from the Banner of Truth publications, whose first magazine was published in 1955, (the year following the experience here recorded), and through the ministry of Doctor Martyn Lloyd Jones. There were some then, and some still now, who were convinced that all that was necessary was to return to a systematic preaching of these doctrines, and then God would send revival.

I am told that the same year saw the beginning of what is now called the Charismatic movement, as differing from Pentecostal churches, but that it was not until the early 1970's that it expanded. Also in the mid seventies there was a greater awareness among non-conformists generally of the importance of the doctrine of the church. The prominence given to this doctrine was followed by a concern for an experience of the truth in the heart, and a return to the New Testament pattern of church life. There are now thousands of churches composed of baptised, regenerate believers throughout the world, as well as many charasmatic fellowships. This re-awakening of an experimental religion was also hailed by some as the hoped for revival, but as the years pass by and the unbelieving masses remain untouched, it is becoming more and more evident that there needs to be a greater movement of the Spirit of God than we have yet seen.

Often, both in personal conversation and in preaching, have I spoken of this persuasion given me at that time. Forty years seemed a long time away in 1954, now there are only a few years left; and I still hope to live to see "greater things than these."

That hope was strengthened several years later as I studied Matthew 24 in the light of the great events which took place when the nation of Israel gained control of Jerusalem in 1967. Jesus says here to his disciples, "There shall not be left here one stone upon another, that shall not be thrown down", and they asked, "Tell us, when shall these things be? and what shall be the sign of thy coming, and of the end of the world?"

Jesus answered as though they had asked three different questions, and concerning the first, said, "This generation shall not pass, till all these things be fulfilled." The generation to which Jesus belonged reached the allotted span of life in AD 70, the year Jerusalem was destroyed. Not one stone was left upon another thirty-seven to forty years after Jesus spoke these prophetic words. According to Luke 21, he also gave them the sign which would indicate that day was near at hand: "When you see Jerusalem surrounded by armies, then know its desolation is near." The temporary withdrawing of the Roman army gave those who heeded his words an opportunity to escape from impending doom

The second question, "What shall be the sign of thy coming?" is answered more fully in Luke's account, especially in Luke 21 v24: "Jerusalem shall be trodden down of the Gentiles, until the times of the Gentiles be fulfilled." A similar term, "fulness of the Gentiles", is used in Romans 11 v25, in which chapter the Holy Spirit uses the analogy of grafting to foretell that the Jews, who for the most part have been by-passed by the gospel, would again be received into God's blessing, like a graft of a true olive being grafted in again to its own stock. This would be as life from the dead, both for them and for the mainly Gentile church.

There can be no doubt that Jesus' words in Luke 21 v24, "And they shall fall by the edge of sword, and they shall be led away captive into all nations:" refer to the dispersal of the Jews following the destruction of Jerusalem by the Romans, and foretold by Moses in Deuteronomy 28 v64-68: "And the LORD shall scatter thee among all people, from one end of the earth to the other; ... And among these nations thou shalt find no ease, neither shall the sole of thy foot have rest;" etc.

There are many scriptures, including the one just referred to, which foretell Israel being restored, and once more becoming a nation in the land of Palestine: e.g. Ezekiel 36 v21-38. The fulfilment of the second part of Luke 21 v24, "and Jerusalem shall be trodden down of the Gentiles, <u>until the times of the Gentiles are fulfilled</u>", is spoken of by Jesus as a sign of his coming. The return of the Jews to the land of Palestine, setting up an Israeli State, and the more recent deliverance of Jerusalem from its Gentile domination in 1967, are now historical facts. They are in themselves another evidence that God is working out his purpose among the nations of the earth.

Carrying forward from Matthew 24 the thought of the generation which saw Jesus' words concerning the destruction of Jerusalem fulfilled, and adding 37-40 years to 1967, brings us to the middle of the third twenty year period mentioned earlier, and about the time when, God willing, I shall be 82. This is, to say the least, a remarkable coincidence.

Likewise there can be no doubt but that Romans 11 foretells the same event as that foretold by Zechariah 12 v10: "And I will pour upon the house of David, and upon the inhabitants of Jerusalem, the spirit of grace and of supplications: and they shall look upon me whom they have pierced, and shall mourn for him, as one mourneth for his only son..." As has already been mentioned this also is linked with the term "fulness of the Gentiles", and an unprecedented revival of the Church of God. This does not give Israel <u>as a nation</u> a place in the plan of God for the future, but a removal of their blindness, and a receiving them into the New Covenant blessing, as the whole passage in Romans 11 states. They failed to fulfil God's ideal of a perfect state, and the mainly Gentile Church has equally failed in its witness over the past 2,000 years, but who can doubt that a tremendous impact would be made by the indigenous Jews in every land, if they became ambassadors for their once-rejected Messiah, the Lord Jesus Christ? Is it not possible that Pentecost was the former rain for the sowing of the seed, and that there will be a latter rain before the final harvest?

This is not the place to attempt to interpret the prophecies concerning all nations being gathered against Israel, and a divine intervention saving them from destruction, as foretold in Zechariah, and in Ezekiel 39. Indeed I have always maintained that the prophetic portions of the Bible can only be fully understood as the events themselves unfold in history - they are the "mysteries hid from the beginning in God".

There are however two thoughts I would drop into the reader's mind. Please bear in mind that these thoughts are only examples of how prophecies, which seemed incapable of fulfilment fifty years ago, are now seen to be realistic. In making these prophetic statements God has only made his purpose known, and the timing and means are often different from what we may think.

First, what destruction and desolation would be caused if every nuclear warhead in the enemy's possession were detonated in situ, either by divine intervention or as a desperate final bid for survival by the Israelis. (In these days of international computer hacking such a thing appears to me no less feasible than the "Star Wars" programme which aims to destroy them in flight after launching).

Secondly, for the first time in history we saw in the Gulf Crisis all nations acting together against one nation which has stepped out of line (Iraq). Surely the stage is being set for the fulfilment of these prophetic passages, even though we cannot understand fully what is meant by them. Today the possibility of the United Nations being 'gathered together against Jerusalem' is very real, especially if

Israel pursues a territorial expansionist policy. Jerusalem is the holy place for Judaism, Islam and Christianity, and the likelihood of the city being divided up by United Nations resolution, is another way in which the prophecies in Zechariah might be fulfilled. One thing is clear: the Lord Jesus has told us, "And when these things <u>begin to come to pass</u>, then look up, and lift up your heads, for your redemption draweth nigh.... Verily I say to you, <u>this generation shall not pass away, till all be fulfilled.</u> Heaven and earth shall pass away: but my words shall not pass away"(Luke 21 v28-33).

Abraham asked God for a sign of possessing the promises made to him. These included the coming of the One in whom all nations of the earth would be blessed, the Lord Jesus Christ. "How shall I know?" he asked. The birth of Isaac was surely the tangible proof that God would fulfil all his word to Abraham, but many years elapsed before Christ came. I believe in these scriptures the Lord has told us of the <u>sign</u> of his coming, that which will reveal the certainty of that event as clearly as the birth of Isaac was a guarantee of his first advent, but not <u>when</u> he will come.

The third question Jesus answered was "...and of the end of the world?" - the last great day when Christ shall come to judge the quick and the dead. Of that event Jesus said there will be no foretelling sign. He spoke of many signs that would be fulfilled before that day, and at that momentous event. Also many indications of the conditions that would prevail at the time of his coming. We are exhorted to watch and pray because many of these features will be present throughout the whole period of these last days, sometimes more prevalent than others. Every generation of believers therefore needs to be on their guard, as men that wait for their Lord. Of that day itself there will be no warning, "...of that day and hour knoweth no man, no, not the angels in heaven, but my Father only." That will be as sudden and all revealing as a flash of lightning, and "in such an hour as ye think not." (Matthew 24 v36-39.)

If the wonderful events foretold in Romans 11 are fulfilled in world-wide revival between 1994 and 2015, then I believe this strange experience, the strong persuasion which has meant so much to me, and of which I have so often spoken, will be seen to have been a vision; if not, only a dream.

"And it shall come to pass in the last days, saith God,... your young men shall see visions, and your old men shall dream dreams." I sometimes wonder if the dreams we old men now dream are about what might have been, if only we had obeyed more fully the vision of our youth. Paul could say, "I was not disobedient to the heavenly vision." God grant that the young men of today may serve him more fully and obediently than I and my generation have done.

## CHAPTER 8
## REHOBOTH

TUCKED AWAY behind the Church of King Charles the Martyr, which is situated on the edge of the famous Pantiles in the town of Tunbridge Wells, Kent, stands a typical and beautiful example of 19th. century Nonconformist architecture named Rehoboth Baptist Chapel. It was given this name, meaning "The Lord hath made room for us", by the Particular Baptist congregation who built it, because of the remarkable way that the site had been made available to them.

After I had been preaching among the churches for about three years, I was asked to preach there on two Sunday mornings. An itinerante minister, Mr. Clement Wood, was the corresponding deacon, and he explained that in the evenings they were supplied by a local pastor from Matfield. This was a very happy arrangement for me, as it enabled me to return to my home church for the rest of the day.

I well remember my first visit, when I spoke from 1 Corinthians 2 v2, "For I determined not to know any thing among you, save Jesus Christ, and him crucified." Although not feeling great liberty in preaching, I was conscious that the power of God was attending the reading of the Word, (I was later to find that there were divisions in that church similar to those in the church at Corinth.)

Soon after this Mr. Wood received a call to become pastor of Tamworth Road Baptist Chapel in Croydon. I was preaching again at Rehoboth one Sunday morning, from Philippians 1 v6, "He which hath begun a good work in you will perform it until the day of Jesus Christ," when in the course of the sermon I mentioned that when one godly, gracious man was taken from a church, the Lord would raise up another that His work should continue. This, I felt, the Lord had done for the church at Rehoboth, in bringing among them a schoolmaster

Rehoboth Chapel.

One of the first practical changes I made as pastor was to remove the over-grown laurels, and plant roses and other flowers. At a later date the steps and entrance were remodelled as in this picture.

Mr. George Rose, who had taken up the heavy burden of work laid down by Mr. Wood. But even as I spoke those words the thought shot into my mind, "Suppose it were you who should be raised up to carry on the Lord's work here."

Nothing was said to me by anyone, but I had a very strong feeling that the Lord had a work for me to do in Tunbridge Wells. I was to learn later that when the three deacons met in the vestry after the service, one of them, Mr. D. Boarer, said, "When he was preaching, it came to me, 'Arise, anoint him; this is he.'" The other two professed to have had similar feelings.

Perhaps I ought to explain that there was a common agreement among the churches I served that all engagements made between corresponding deacons or secretaries and the visiting ministers were agreed as from the first of July for the following year. This had come about because some ministers were engaged to preach two or three years ahead, and many churches found it difficult to obtain the preacher they wanted for the Lord's Day.

I had three full Sundays of of preaching at Rehoboth scheduled for 1961, but in May of that year I received a letter from the secretary asking whether I could give nine extra Sundays for the following year. I felt sure, although nothing was said in the letter, that my presentiments about being asked to become pastor were correct. It had always been my practice when receiving letters before the usual time to acknowledge their receipt and say I would reply later. In this instance, I replied by saying I did not feel able to take any Sundays from other churches and give them to Rehoboth, and there I thought the matter would rest.

It was not to be so, for two weeks before the 'deadline' of the first of July I received another letter inviting me to preach at Rehoboth with a view to becoming the pastor. That letter sent me to the Throne of Grace as perhaps never before, and I spent a night in prayer and tears, asking God to make plain to me his will. Very early in the morning I picked up my Bible and read in Revelation 3 v8, "Behold, I have set before thee an open door, and no man can shut it," I realised that this was a very suitable word, but it did not grip my soul with the power that would convince me it was a word from the Lord. While it is true that we may take any and every promise of God to be relied upon, when we seek a word of personal direction in some specific matter, I believe there needs to be the witness of the Spirit with our spirit that this is the word of the Lord for the occasion.

As I went out to my work about 5 o'clock in the morning, I thought of how a former pastor of Tamworth Road (another George Rose)had been given the word, "Take this child and nurse it for me, and I will give thee thy wages." (He used to say that he knew this would not be a lifelong pastorate, but as Moses was handed over to another when weaned, so it would be with himself and the church there.) I prayed that the Lord would, if it were his will, give me such a word that I also might discern his will in the matter. When I came in for my breakfast, I picked up my Bible and sitting down in a chair prayed, "Lord, direct me to a word that will show me thy will." I opened my Bible on the first book of Chronicles, chapter 22, and the first words my eyes lighted on were:

"Now, my son, the Lord be with thee: and prosper thou, and build the house of the Lord thy God, as he hath said of thee. Only the Lord give thee wisdom and understanding, and give thee charge concerning Israel, that thou mayest keep the law of the Lord thy God. Then shalt thou prosper, if thou takest heed to fulfil the statutes and judgements which the Lord charged Moses with concerning Israel: BE STRONG, AND OF GOOD COURAGE; DREAD NOT, NOR BE DISMAYED."

I felt my whole body tremble under the impact of that word. It came as a word of direction, a word from the Lord. My heart went up to him in thankfulness, and yet in fear; fear because the work was great; thankfulness for the encouragement given, "be strong and of good courage, dread not, nor be dismayed." That moment is so clearly etched in my memory that I see every detail of the scene in my mind's eye even as I write these words thirty years later.

All that day I was conscious that the Spirit of God was with me in a marked way. At our breakfast reading, my wife read from 1 Peter 5:

The elders which are among you I exhort, who also am an elder, and a witness of the sufferings of Christ, and also a partaker of the glory that shall be revealed. Feed the flock of God which is among you, taking the oversight thereof, not by constraint, but willingly; not for filthy lucre, but of a ready mind. Neither as being lords over God's heritage, but being ensamples to the flock. And when the chief Shepherd shall appear, ye shall receive a crown of glory that fadeth not away.

This also came as a clear direction from God, for the reading was not deliberately chosen, but more was to follow. The Daily Light portion for the day was the word given to Pastor George Rose, about which I had already prayed, "Take this child and nurse it for me." In many ways that day, I felt the Lord had given me clear leading, far beyond my greatest expectation, but the greatest confirmation of all was yet to come.

Two days later, still feeling the effect of all this upon my spirit, I went out early in the morning, right away from every other person, sat down on a bale of hay, and wrote a letter accepting that invitation to "preach with a view." Only after I had posted it did I speak to my father, who would of course be very much involved in the consequences which would follow. He replied by saying, "David, I will tell you something of which I have never before breathed a word to anyone. When Billie [my elder brother] was so desperately ill as a child and his life despaired of, I felt these words given me concerning him, 'he shall not die but live, and declare the wonderful works of God.' And he was, as you know, wonderfully restored." Then he went on to say, "Though at one time I thought much about the ministry, the Lord has never called me to it, but he impressed upon my mind these words, 'Behold, a son shall be born to thee, he shall build a house for my name.' I thought at that time that Billie would be healed and become a minister of the gospel, but I see now those words concerned you."

The words which my father quoted immediately preceded the words in 1 Chron. 22 9-10. The whole text reads: "Behold, a son shall be born to thee, who shall be a man of rest; and I will give him rest from all his enemies round about; for his name shall be Solomon, and I will give peace and quietness unto Israel in his days. He shall build a house for my name..." This answered a question which was in my mind: what is meant by "as he hath said of thee"? (page 86). Did that relate to the open door spoken of in Revelation 3? How wonderful it appeared to me that this promise was given to my father just before I was born!

In medieval times there was a custom known as "breaking gold", as a pledge, or means of confirming the authenticity of a messenger. A brooch or similar gold object was broken, and one half given to each party in the contract or whatever business was in hand. At a subsequent meeting each produced his half, and as the two pieces were seen to fit together, so the genuine nature of the message or person was established. That day my father and I stood in holy awe and amazement as we saw the two pieces of gold come together and fit so perfectly. I could take anyone to the exact spot on the farm where this discussion took place.

On the first Sunday in July I administered the Lord's Supper at Rehoboth for the first time, and approached that communion service with the thought that if this is really of the Lord it will be right at his Table; if it is not right there, it will not be right at all. Not only did I feel comfortable in my own mind that the Lord's blessing was upon us that day, but during the week I met a person that had been present on that occasion, who said to me, "I feel sure it is right, because it was so right at the Lord's Table."

When, in January 1962, the time came for me to preach as 'Pastor Elect', I was very apprehensive, and thankful that I had not been asked to preach every Sunday for three consecutive months as was usually the case, but a total of thirteen Sundays during the first six months. I was not happy with my own preaching at Rehoboth, neither had I preached there many times, and was fearful about preaching to the same people every week. However, at the end of the first period of five weeks, I felt a real sadness in my heart that I was not going there again the next Lord's Day. During that probational period I was encouraged to know that some members who had previously said they "heard me with pleasure, but not with power" were being blessed through the word.

There was also an incident of the Lord's providential goodness on the farm which encouraged me at that time. I have often observed in my life that if there is little hay made in the summer, this is usually followed by a "green winter", in which case less hay is needed for the cattle. On the other hand, when summer grass and hay are plentiful, a long winter follows. This is all part of God's wonderful plan in the balance of nature.

During the previous summer, we had made far more hay than ever before, but as the winter wore on many farmers were forced to buy hay, and the price rose accordingly. One of these was a man who

A Load of Mischief.

Taken on a Whit Monday at Plumey Feather Farm, where the cows were kept, and the Sunday School gatherings took place. The hay barn and hayracks mentioned on page 91 can be seen to the right of the picture. I am driving the tractor.

had just taken a small farm on the edge of Broadwater Forest, between Groombridge and Tunbridge Wells, and he asked if I could supply him with hay. He had not had opportunity to make hay for himself and could not afford the merchant's price of over £20 a ton. After carefully assessing what we had in stock and how much we would need, I sold him all that could be spared at £11 a ton.

Soon after this had taken place, another small farmer, who was a member of the same church as myself in Crowborough, turned up with a tractor and trailer. He reminded me that I had promised that if ever he was in difficulty I would help where I could, and then he went on to say, "When I came by the other day I could see you had plenty of hay left, so I've come over to see if you could let me have some." This put me in a quandary, because I knew we might be in danger of not having sufficient for ourselves; but in the end I let him have two loads. It was understood on both sides that there would be no need of payment.

Again I made a careful assessment, and decided that if we rationed the cows to sixteen bales of hay a day between them, this would see us through to the end of March. Often by the first of April there was sufficient grass growing in the fields to feed the cows, and I hoped that our needs would be met.

I ought to explain that I never "kept my cows in" during the winter, although a covered yard was available should they need it. Our ground was well drained, and some cows preferred to lie out, even in the snow, and I believe were all the healthier for it. I had erected a covered way alongside the hay barn, with hay racks all along its length, so that hay could be placed directly into them for free access by the cows. We also grew a lot of winter vegetables, especially sprouts, and when these were picked for sale to local shops, the cows were allowed to graze over the area behind an electric fence, and clear up the waste leaves and stalks.

On the morning of the first of April I stood in the hay barn. There in the middle of the floor was a pitiful little pile of hay, just sufficient for one day's ration, and as yet very little in the fields for the cows to eat. The small acreage of rye which I grew for an "early bite" and subsequent harvesting had already been devoured, and forty pairs of hungry eyes were looking at me reproachfully over the top of empty hay racks. I have always tried to follow the motto of Psalm 37 v3, but that morning the Devil quoted it back to me; "Trust in the Lord and do good; so shalt thou dwell in the land, and verily thou shalt be fed." It was as though he was saying, "<u>Your cows need hay, not just words.</u>"

However, things were not, I thought, as bad as they looked, for I knew a Christian farmer in nearby Hartfield who had told me that although he sold hay he always kept back two thousand bales in case next year's haymaking season was difficult. So I phoned him, explaining my predicament. I was shattered when he said, "If only you had let me know a few days ago, I could have helped you; but the price is so good I've sold all I can spare." He very kindly promised to bring me over enough for <u>two days</u> and charge me only £11 a ton - the same price at which I had previously sold.

What was I to do? For a moment or two I stood hesitating before reaching for the Directory to look for a hay merchant; then the phone rang. It was a call from a farmer near Lewes, deacon of the little Barcombe chapel, a man greatly beloved, and who had taken me into his family as if I were a son. After a few preliminary greetings, he said, "David, are you short of hay?" Cautiously I enquired why he should think such a thing, to which he replied, "The Lord laid it on my mind this morning that you might be. If you are, we would be pleased to send you a lorry load as a gift from the Lord." I then felt free to tell him what had happened, and how at that very moment I was wondering what to do. He went on to say they could not send immediately, but that it would be there in two day's time.

On replacing the phone, I picked up my Bible and opening it at random found that my eye lighted on the text - yes, I expect you've guessed it! "Trust in the Lord and do good; so shalt thou dwell in the land, and verily thou shalt be fed." I read on until verse 25: "I have been young, and now am old; yet I have not seen the righteous forsaken, nor his seed begging bread. He is ever merciful, and lendeth..." I fell on my knees and worshipped the Lord saying, "O God, thou art my God." I was sure that the Lord had provided my cows with hay as surely as he fed the children of Israel with manna. This was a great encouragement to me when I was so fearful that I would not be able to feed the flock of God at Rehoboth. I knew that this same God had promised to feed his people with food convenient for them, and that he would honour his word.

In a few days the weather changed dramatically, as it can in the spring, and soon there was an abundance of feed in the fields, so that the "gift from the Lord" was sufficient for our needs. I find it difficult to understand how anyone can consider this sequence of events without acknowledging the overruling hand of God and his perfect timing. Had my friend at Barcombe phoned five minutes earlier, I would not have known my other friend's reserves were gone; had he phoned five minutes later, in all probability I would have agreed to purchase from a merchant. As it was, I had the two days supply to see me through to the arrival of the gift. Hezekiah said, "By these things men live; and in all these things is the life of my spirit", and David tells us, "Whoso is wise, and will observe these things, even they shall understand the loving kindness of the Lord."

In due time I received a call from the church to become pastor. It was not unanimous, and there were some objections to the matter being done too hastily, but I felt confident that this was the will of God and accepted without delay. From early July, as "pastor designate", I began to take prayer meetings and midweek services, and to chair evenings when there were representatives from various Christian organisations speaking. My wife and I also began a "Handicraft Club", where we gathered together the children from all three Strict Baptist churches in Tunbridge Wells. making articles for sale on behalf of the Leprosy Mission.

On 15th. December a special meeting was held at which, after the deacon George Rose had given an account of the church's leadings, I gave a testimony of my call by grace, my call to the ministry, and my call to the pastorate, and I shall conclude this chapter by quoting the closing words of that testimony, taken verbatim from a tape recording:

"My friends, the Lord knows that above all things I desire to be a man of rest and peace, and God knows I don't speak disparagingly, but it is rest and peace and quietness which is needed in this church, as in every other church; and it is my earnest prayer that God will keep me and enable me to set my heart and mind to serve the Lord, and that he will fulfil this word here in this place, and build an house for his name here. There is no need for me to go into details, but because the meeting called to invite me to preach with a view to the pastorate was called hurriedly, there was opposition here in some ways, and the Lord quieted my mind concerning it. I was rather troubled because the meeting was called contrary to the rules, but a word was given me which you will find in 2 Chron. 30 v18, the prayer of Hezekiah: "And Hezekiah prayed for them saying, The good Lord pardon every one that prepareth his heart to seek God, the Lord God of his fathers, though he be not cleansed according to the purification of the sanctuary." That pointed me to this, that though things were not done in the right order, yet they were overruled by our gracious God. Mr. Leslie Rowell recently took those words here; he preached in this chapel; these matters were entirely unknown to him, but I said to him afterwards that, had he known, he could not have spoken more appropriately than he did that night.

There was a time when I felt great rebellion in my heart about coming here. I once said to a friend outside, "I find it hard to preach at Rehoboth." One of the things which tried me was that I did not feel to love this cause with an overwhelming love; I did not feel to have preached the word with power here as I felt the Lord had helped me in other places. I thought, "Well, surely, if it is the Lord's will that I should come here, I should not feel this. Why should the Lord send me here? Why could I not go to some place where I should feel nothing but love?" (no reflection on our friends here, but this is how I felt). That night, I came into the prayer meeting and after the meeting I went to the home of one of our friends. I went home in a very different frame of mind. I felt indeed that the Lord had a work for me here, and I believe he has; only I pray that he will answer the prayer which you have sung this evening in that opening hymn.\* I do thank you, because I feel that it came from your hearts. So from that day until now, I have felt increasing help and increasing love to this place.

So I have come feeling that this is the way, but I would not be quite open and honest if I did not say there was a word which tried me very sorely at the beginning of the year: "I will overturn, overturn, overturn it, until he come whose right it is." I wondered if that applied to me here, and that impression was deepened when my pastor preached here on 7th. January and quoted these words, "I will overturn, overturn, overturn it." The outcome of this exercise on my soul was this, "Lord, even if it is thy purpose that I should labour here that another might come and build the house, even as David prepared for Solomon, so let it be". I felt content that it should be as he willed it.

Early in my ministry I had this word, "One shall sow and another shall reap." The general interpretation of that has been that one sows the word and another reaps from it. The Lord Jesus said to his disciples, "Other men have laboured, and ye have entered into their labours." Knowing my own heart, how prone one is to be taken away with self-esteem and pride, I said, "Lord, if it is to be one or the other, make me a sower." Now I find it in my heart that God would make me both a sower, and a reaper here. That we might find indeed, that they who sow in tears shall reap in joy, both in the pulpit and in the pew."
*That hymn was Gadsby's, 373:

With heavenly power, O Lord, defend,
Him whom we now to thee commend;
His person bless, his soul secure;
And make him to the end endure.

Gird him with all-sufficient grace;
Direct his feet in paths of peace;
Thy truth and faithfulness fulfil
And help him to obey thy will.

Before him thy protection send;
O love him, save him to the end!
Nor let him as thy pilgrim rove
Without the convoy of thy love.

Enlarge, inflame and fill his heart;
In him thy mighty power exert;
That thousands, yet unborn, may praise
The wonders of redeeming grace.

## CHAPTER 9
## NEW BEGINNINGS and THE WAY AHEAD

IN THE previous chapter, quoting from a recording of my testimony to the church given after accepting the pastorate and before actually taking up office, I mentioned telling a friend, "I find it hard to preach at Rehoboth." This dear brother was a man of forthright nature, and he later challenged me with, "If you find it hard to preach here, why ever are you thinking about becoming the pastor?" My reply was equally simple and frank: "Because I do not want to be a Jonah."

It has always been my belief that one of the most important things in the life of a believer is to know the will of God and have the courage to do it, even though it may not be one's own heart wish, or be in accordance with the desires and advice of others.

In the early days of my ministry this lesson was brought home to me with startling clarity. I had begun to preach regularly, Sundays and weekdays, at a small town on the Sussex coast. Although I was not actively seeking a pastorate, it is doubtless in the mind of all itinerating ministers that perhaps it may be the Lord's will that they may be called to pastor a flock. Indeed, I believe such a desire is right and scriptural. In this instance, there were a number of things which made this particular place attractive to me: I had close relatives who were worshipping there; I had liberty and joy in preaching the word; it was a church with a good history; and to my natural mind it was very attractive because I love my native county and I love the sea.

Although nothing had been said to me by any member of the church, this impression became one day so great upon my mind that I prayed, "Lord, if it is thy will for me to go to Hastings, give me especial liberty in the pulpit when I go to preach this next Sunday; if not, close my mouth." I found my heart longing that it would be the former, and in fact was confident it would be so, especially as I found great liberty in meditating on John 3 v16.

Thirty-three years later I was asked by one who was present on that Sunday, "Do you remember the day you sat down a few minutes after giving out your text? Nobody seemed to know what to do. We wondered if the deacon would give out the last hymn and close the service. I'm sure everybody in the chapel was praying for you; and then, after what seemed an age, you stood up and went on preaching as though nothing had happened!"

Did I remember! Could I ever forget? I don't remember going on to preach as though nothing had happened, but that day has never left me, and I am conscious that each time I stand up in God's name my total dependence must be upon him. I have often said, "If God gives me the skeleton of a sermon, he will clothe it with flesh and life, but if I make one, that's all it will ever be - a skeleton!"

As all the church members involved in that church have since died, I was able to tell this brother not only the reason why my mouth had been closed, but something I later discovered which threw light upon that painful experience. There came a time when I was visiting an old lady who lived in a little village a few miles inland from Hastings, when she suddenly asked me, "Did you ever receive an invitation to be our pastor?" I assured her that nobody had ever mentioned such a thing, let alone given me a letter of invitation. "That's strange," she said, "There was a unanimous vote at a church meeting to ask the deacon to write and invite you, but we never heard any more about it." Nothing more was said on the subject, but I thought I knew what had happened to that letter - it was in the pocket of the deacon on that Sunday! He had probably prayed along similar lines as I had done, that he might be absolutely sure before giving me that invitation. I believe God overruled in the matter, but needless to say, I have never again prayed that sort of prayer! It was many years before I could face preaching again from John 3 v16.

On one occasion when preaching at Rehoboth, I recounted how the Lord had answered my prayer over a practical problem. If I remember correctly, it was about when we were haymaking, and the rain was sweeping across the countryside threatening every moment to burst upon us. Then torrential rain came so close that the men making hay in the next field had to stop and run for shelter, but in a miraculous way it stopped short of the boundary hedge. Not until we had got the last load home did it rain, and then I was soaked to the skin while tying down a waterproof cover on the haystack.

On the day following mentioning this answer to prayer I was at work on the farm, when I received a visit from the brother who once questioned my coming to a church where I found it hard to preach. He came straight to the point, and said, "Dave, at one time I prayed that if it was the Lord's will he would do something to stop you from coming to Rehoboth. Now I hope and pray that you _will_ come; I want to know the God you know, the God who does things _today_, not just two hundred or two thousand years ago!" That was particularly encouraging to me, because at the very time he came in, I was being sorely tempted by the enemy of souls that in giving a personal testimony I was talking about myself instead of preaching Christ.

Many of my friends, on being called to the ministry or to a pastorate, have felt that it was essential to give up all secular work, but I did not feel this to be necessary. Quite apart from my obligations to my ageing parents and afflicted brother ("If any man provide not for his own house, he hath denied the faith and is worse than an unbeliever"), I had always found that my most profitable times of study were in the field. There, while working alone in the open air, or alone in the early

Ploughing with Prince in the furrow

morning milking the cows, I enjoyed much of the presence of the Lord and leading of the Holy Spirit. The Lord was pleased to bring to my mind passages of scripture relevant to whatever subject was on my mind, so that I could say I had a Bible study, even without a Bible. The healthy physical exercise also gave me strength and mental alertness, which was to continue to be an asset in the days ahead. Often as I worked in the field I would have a notebook in my pocket and jot down thoughts as they came into my mind. My late pastor had encouraged me in this by saying, "Thoughts come to my mind like birds to a tree; if I don't catch them while they are there, they are quickly gone and I cannot recall them." Many a poem likewise was composed, especially for use as recitations at Sunday School meetings.

Other factors also made me feel that my life was not one to be spent in a study among the great theological books of the old divines. My lack of education and natural aptitudes made such a course difficult, but that no doubt could have been overcome. Perhaps the greatest reason of all was my first experience of commentaries! Soon after I began to preach my pastor gave me a few books by Doctor Barnes. "You will find these useful, David," he said, "but you will soon realise that he was an ardent exponent of infant baptism, and brings the subject in wherever there is an opportunity." My immediate reaction was, "If I cannot trust the man's judgement on such a simple thing as baptism, how can I be expected to trust it in more difficult matters?"

As I gathered more books, I found more and more conflicting views, ably argued by eminent and godly men, and came to the conclusion that after studying them all I did not know what were my own thoughts, what were just the thoughts of others, or if I truly had the mind of the Spirit. It is good to read what other men have written, including those with whom we differ. By doing so we come to know what they believe and have experienced, but the book which tells us what God has said is the Bible. To this we must go for our instruction, for it is the all-sufficient and infallible Word of God.

These things made me feel that in my case it was the Lord's will for me to continue my secular calling, which would enable me to serve the church without being a financial burden, and to continue my former practice of study.

In order to devote more time to pastoral duties I further reduced the area given over to fruit and market garden crops. Later I gave up the thousand head flock of laying hens which up until that point I had managed 'in my spare time'. Despite this large reduction in income, the Lord prospered my business. I learned from him the lesson learnt by a merchant who demurred about taking up an appointment as an Ambassador under Queen Elizabeth the first; "You look after my business," she said, "and I will look after yours." By her patronage of his business he gained much financially, and in my business I also proved that "God is no man's debtor".

In my testimony to the church, I had spoken of my commission "to build the house of the Lord as he hath said". In my early discussions with the deacons about becoming pastor, I requested a copy of the Trust Deed, in which I found that the chapel was built for the worship of God according to the beliefs of the Particular Baptist Denomination, and in which baptism by immersion was required prior to admittance to the Lord's Table.

I believe that the Holy Spirit is as sovereign in the life of the church as in the life of the believer, and that he had a purpose in leading little groups of believers, who in various places studied the Bible for the foundation of their individual churches, to make each church unique. As with the work in the hearts of individual believers, so in the churches: unity without uniformity; basically the same, yet no two exactly alike. Therefore, any attempt to stamp upon churches one uniform set of doctrinal statements, however commendable the intention, is not good, and if possible, every church should stand upon its original foundations. I was delighted to find that both the active deacons were more than willing for me to follow this course at Rehoboth.

Having accepted the call to become pastor, I was faced with a new dilemma on the home front. If I were to give full time to the Lord's work, I needed a full time cowman on the farm; but as I had promised a retired farmworker and his wife the use of the little old farm cottage in which I was brought up (and to which I retired when 65), I was hesitant about advertising for one, as we had no accommodation to offer. After prayerful thought I placed the matter in the Lord's hands and asked him to send us a cowman before the first of January.

On Christmas Eve, I answered a knock on the door and opened to a stranger, who said, "You're looking for a cowman I believe." He came in and we discussed the situation. Although he had no previous experience with cows, he was ready to learn, and confident of being able to cope. When faced with the housing situation, he said, "Oh, something is sure to turn up; meanwhile I can live with my brother-in-law down the road." So at the very last moment we were provided with a cowman, and he began his duties the same week that I took up mine as pastor.

This man, Charlie Brooks, was with me for many years and made a first class cowman. He was an excellent worker and soon took over completely the responsibility for the herd. About this time I dropped the pedigree status, simply keeping to a pure-bred Guernsey line. I was later amazed to find that Charlie and I were related through our great grandfathers, his own mother being an Obbard. He was also provided with a cottage almost immediately, for I wrote to the landlord of the rented farm and he allowed me the use of the nearest cottage on his estate rent-free, on condition I surrendered it at a month's notice.

After a few years I received such notice on a Saturday, and put the matter from my mind, so that it would not disturb my peace or preaching on the Sunday. On the Monday morning, the old chap in our cottage came to me with the key, saying that as his wife needed more attention than he could give, they would be going to live with one of their daughters, and no longer needed the accommodation. Just one more example of the perfect timing of our God.

There were a number of problems in the church at Rehoboth, some directly related to my being called to the pastorate, and one deacon, Mr. Boarer, resigned because of them. This left only the senior deacon, Mr. Archibald Cox, now confined to his home; Mr. John Buckland, a dear gracious man, filled with the love of Christ, but without administrative gifts; and the able, younger deacon, George Rose. In the last man I found a brother much of my own age and persuasions, and often, as we spoke of all the difficulties ahead, I would say to my wife, "Still, we've got George Rose."

On the last Friday of 1962 George, John and I stayed behind after the prayer meeting for further prayer and fellowship. There was real spiritual love and joy in our hearts as we parted that night in anticipation of sharing in fellowship and blessing in the years to come, following the commencement of my pastorate on the first Sunday of the New Year.

Heavy snow fell the following day, and about 7.30 that Saturday night George Rose was found dead on the chapel steps. He had suffered a massive heart attack as he was clearing snow from the chapel steps ready for the Sunday services. It was a tragic loss and devastating blow for us all, especially for his wife and three young boys.

As all rail and road traffic was heavily disrupted on that last Sunday of the year, and I could not travel to the chapel where I was engaged to preach, I came to Rehoboth. As the man who had been expected there was also unable to get through,

I preached, taking Psalm 121 v1-2 as my text: "I will lift up mine eyes unto the hills; from whence cometh my help? My help cometh from the Lord, which made heaven and earth" - a text not only suitable for the occasion, but expressing my own feelings then and throughout the twenty years in which I was to serve the church as pastor.

By the time my pastorate actually commenced, the prediction, "I will overturn, overturn, overturn it," was already evidently being brought about, for my first duty was to conduct the funerals of two deacons, Mr. Cox, the senior deacon, having also passed away. In this time of distress and trial I was helped by two promises which had been given me, neither as yet having been mentioned, either to the church or in this book. Indeed they were promises which I knew must be locked up in my heart until such time as the Lord should be pleased to make them manifest to others, and openly.

The first was given to me through my pastor, Stanley Delves. He had been baptised by Mr. Evans at Rehoboth, but left the church there to become pastor at Forest Fold, Crowborough, before pastor Evans resigned and formed a separate church in Grove Hill Hall not far away. Mr. Delves had a great love and esteem for Mr. Evans, and knew that the good man's trouble at Rehoboth sprang from not being able to give whole-hearted assent to certain doctrinal statements which had been imposed upon the original articles. He was fearful that I too would face difficulties over these added articles.

One day he said to me, "David, the Lord has quieted my mind about you going to Rehoboth with these words, 'thou shalt be called, The repairer of the breach, The restorer of paths to dwell in.'" Although it was at that time his personal wish that I should follow in his steps at Forest Fold - he had on two separate occasions asked if I would become co-pastor with him - he was now fully persuaded that God would use me in some way to bring about peace between the then sharply divided churches of Rehoboth and Grove Hill. He said he hoped to live and see the day when reconciliation was made and one new church formed.

The other promise came from Ezekiel 37, a chapter which I have often read for my own soul's refreshment and to stimulate prayer for revival. One day the words in verse 17 struck me with a force and power which seemed overwhelming: "And they shall become one in thine hand." That word did for me what Isaiah 58 v12 had done for my pastor - it gave me personal conviction that God would do at Tunbridge Wells what he has seldom done in the long and chequered history of our denominational life, that is, bring together two churches that had been formed by a split and had continued to show open hostility one to the other.

What did the future hold? How were all these seemingly insurmountable obstacles to be overcome, the difficulties resolved, and the attitudes of mind changed? Two things greatly encouraged me as I faced the future without the help of George Rose, whom I had hoped would give me support.

The first was the promise, "Thou wilt keep him in perfect peace whose mind is stayed on thee." I had read somewhere that the phrase "stayed on thee" could also be interpreted, "Has but one prop in thee". The Lord had permitted one important prop to be removed, but if I was stayed upon him I would be upheld. The margin reads "Rock of Ages" for "everlasting strength", and although weak in myself, I was humbly confident. As a practical man, I knew that one reliable prop put under a weak beam would take all the weight, even though it added no more strength to the beam itself. I was well aware of the truth expressed in these lovely words:

    On the Rock I sometimes tremble,
    Faint of heart and weak of knee;
    But the steadfast Rock of Ages
    NEVER TREMBLES UNDER ME.

The other encouragement was that I knew that the God who gave and fulfilled warnings, was the same God who gave and fulfilled promises. In the commencement of the overturning, I saw there was a guarantee of the final building. This strengthened my own determination to seek to please no person or party, but to "build the house" according to what I believed to be the divine plan.

It was my wish that no great celebration or meeting should be held to mark my induction as pastor, and the church graciously complied with that request. On the first Sunday of January 1963, I preached in the morning, from what text I do not now remember. In the evening the service at my home church in Crowborough was cancelled, and I believe that practically the whole congregation came to Rehoboth, when Mr. Stanley Delves preached, and then received me into fellowship at the Lord's Table. Immediately following this, I, as the pastor, administered the ordinance to the combined church membership. This was a time of sacred communion, and I am thankful to be able to say with all honesty that I never once came to the Lord's Table, in all the years I was pastor, without feeling in my heart some sweetness of the Lord's presence. To me, when the Lord himself presides, the Lord's Table is the most sacred and blessed spot on earth. This is well expressed by the hymn we sometimes sang on those occasions;

Here, O my Lord, I see thee face to face;
Here would I touch and handle things unseen;
Here grasp with firmer hands the eternal grace,
And all my weariness upon thee lean.

Here would I feed upon the bread of God;
Here drink with thee the royal wine of heaven;
Here would I lay aside each earthly load;
Here taste afresh the calm of sin forgiven.

> This is the hour of banquet and of song;
> This is the heavenly table spread for me;
> Here let me feast and feasting still prolong
> The brief, bright hour of fellowship with Thee.

So began a pastorate which was to continue for twenty years in which I saw much of the Lord's goodness, and traced his hand in many things in both providence and grace. In due time it pleased him to bring about a union of the two churches, thus fulfilling the vision I shared with my late pastor, and which I later found to have been the confident hope of others who had prayed for this very thing. I now have the privilege of serving as an elder in the new church, named 'Pantiles Baptist Church', under the leadership of a younger pastor. We have proved that "God moves in a mysterious way his wonders to perform", but the recording of those years must be another story.

# APPENDIX

"IS THIS A STRICT BAPTIST CHAPEL?" This question was asked on the steps of Rehoboth Chapel after the service one Sunday evening in 1938: many heads turned to see the reason for the question. It was provoked by the attendance at the service of a young man in casual clothes, open-necked shirt, and curly hair a little longer than the usual cut. That young man was thankful for the warm reception given by the pastor, Mr. E. A. Brooker: "Pleased to see you, my boy: come again, come again." Little did he realise that young man would "come again, come again" as the pastor for a period of twenty years, for I was the young man in question. Thankfully we record that there can now be few who think a Strict Baptist is defined by what a man wears, how he trims his hair, or what phrases he uses, but the question is still relevant.

Several years ago I was asked to address a women's meeting at the local Salvation Army Citadel. The Brigadier said to me, "Let's see, you have the 'Select Few' at your place, don't you?" I asked what he meant by that, and received the reply, "Well now, if I or Mrs. Brown wanted to come to a service, would we be allowed in?" Unhappily I have found he was not alone in his idea of what a Strict Baptist Church is, and will endeavour to give a simple explanation.

The New Testament concept of a church has nothing to do with a building: the word simply means "a called out assembly". The one true church of Jesus Christ is composed of all true believers (irrespective of where they worship) who have been called out of the world, as Jesus expressed in John 17. A local church is an assembly of believers who are one in Christ, worshipping and witnessing in a certain place. Philippians 1 v1 describes this as consisting of "saints in Christ Jesus" - those who believe in him; "with bishops" (also called elders or pastors) - those who are called of God to care for the spiritual welfare of the church; "and deacons" - those chosen by the believers themselves to care for the material needs of the fellowship. The formation of the first church at Jerusalem is described in Acts 2. It was an organised, autonomous body.

A <u>Baptist</u> Church is one which admits into its membership only those who have been baptised by immersion on confession of their faith. That some Baptist Churches do in fact admit non-baptised believers does not alter the fact that this is the correct definition. We practise baptism by immersion because there is no doubt that the word "BAPTIZO" signifies this. The Greek Orthodox Church still practises immersion as the correct mode.

All Strict Baptist Churches are in agreement over church membership; there can sometimes be a difference of practice toward visitors, or transient communion, but normally it is true that a <u>Strict</u> Baptist Church is one which restricts communion at the Lord's Table to those who have been baptised by immersion. Many 'Free churches' restrict communion to "all who love the Lord", separating it from the Lord's command, "Be baptised every one of you". Others further restrict the table - until recently the Church of England required such a person to be "confirmed, or prepared to be confirmed by the Bishop". Some churches require such a person to be a member of that local church, or of a particular denomination. All restrict the Lord's Table in some way, and while Strict Baptists do not deny others the right to adopt the method they think most appropriate, they themselves feel it right to adhere to the practice of the Apostolic Church as clearly laid down in the Book of Acts.

Anyone visiting a Strict Baptist Church as it "observes the ordinance of Lord's Table" would see exactly the same scene as described by Justin Martyr, A.D.100, in his "Apology" to the Roman Emperor Trajan: "On the day called Sunday believers meet for a service consisting of the reading of the Apostles and Prophets. When the reader has ceased the President instructs and delivers an exhortation. Following a prayer of thanksgiving, the consecrated bread and wine would be distributed among the worshippers, who had to be baptised believers." (This quotation was given me by my pastor, as copied from a book in a Public Library).

Many of these churches were originally known as "Particular Baptists", the name stemming from an early Confession of Faith where reference is made to persons who have been "particularly chosen for salvation". From 1870 onward many churches adopted the term "Strict" to clarify their position regarding the Lord's Table, although the prefix "Strict" was originally given to the churches who did not adopt the 'open table position' by those who did.

When Baptists first began to worship in Tunbridge Wells is not certain. Those in Pembury and Speldhurst joined together in association in 1646, moving into Tunbridge Wells in 1733, and in 1770 a chapel was built on land adjoining Mount Ephraim House. This continued for about thirty years, the last pastor being Joseph Haynes, who died in 1813, after which the building was converted into cottages. Soon after this, mention is made of Baptists meeting for worship in Quarry Road; whether or not this sprang from the Mount Ephraim assembly cannot be discovered, but it is evident that Rehoboth chapel had its origins among the people who attended the Quarry Road meetings.

The chapel was built for a local butcher and lay preacher, Mr. Thomas Edwards. He was a man of great evangelistic zeal, and of whom it is recorded he preached to "Vast concourses of people" on Tunbridge Wells common. The way in which the walls were raised is well described by him in a letter to the editor of the "Earthen Vessel" magazine, 1851:

"We were completely overcome by their liberality; they said nothing, but worked well; it would have rejoiced your heart to have seen them. One of our number is a glazier; he kindly offered to do that department gratis; another is a carpenter; he offered to work simply for his wages without any profit, if we found the materials; another is a sawyer, and he deeply regretted that he had no money, but he said that he would throw off five shillings in the pound for all the sawyer's work that might be required; another poor weather-beaten brother, who knows what short-commons means, said, though he had 'got no money, we must have somebody to dig the foundations', and he said he would cheerfully work a week at it for nothing".

Rehoboth was publicly opened on 3rd September 1851, and all went well for some years, but in 1873 the services terminated, and the chapel was closed. However, one of the Trustees, Mr. Carr, one night dreamed that he said to his son John, "Let us go down to the chapel and ask the Lord to open it again for preaching." He thought his son agreed, so they went down to the chapel, found the doors open, and the building filled with people on their knees in the attitude of prayer. He was so surprised that he said, "My good people, what brings you here?" They all arose and replied, "We want the pure gospel preached to us." Upon this he awoke, and behold it was a dream.

This made a deep impression upon him which was further strengthened when, on visiting a good man who was dying, he was told, "Mr. Carr, I have felt strongly impressed that the chapel will be re-opened and be filled with people; and you will be the man to do it." Mr. Carr was very surprised at what was said, replying, "I shall never do that, I feel myself a poor foolish creature; I could not manage the cause." The dying man said, "I have no doubt the thing will come to pass." These words proved to be prophetic, for the chapel was re-opened on New Years Day, 1874, and has been filled with people many times since then.